Success by Emotions

Success

BY

Emotions

**ACHIEVE THE IMPOSSIBLE
IN HALF THE TIME**

BOB RAYBOULD

Success BY Emotions
PUBLISHING

Success BY Emotions
PUBLISHING

Success by Emotions
Copyright © 2025 by Bob Raybould

All rights reserved. No part of this publication may be reproduced, distributed, or transmitted in any form or by any means, including photocopying, recording, or other electronic or mechanical methods, without the prior written permission of the copyright holder, except in the case of brief quotations embodied in critical reviews and certain other noncommercial uses permitted by copyright law.

Hardcover ISBN: 979-8-218-51119-7
Paperback ISBN: 979-8-218-51120-3

To the patience of my wife, Nancy, and my family as I have exposed and eliminated (and continue to expose and eliminate) my many false ideas. To my many editors who have helped me understand these laws of nature well enough to write a book about them. With especial thanks to my final editor, Anna Krusinski. To those who were able to use these laws before I fully understood them. And, finally, to all who have listened to me as I have tried to articulate my growing understanding of these laws.

Also, to my friend Johnnie Bryant, who is willing to recommend this book based on his successful use of these principles many years ago before I fully understood them.

Contents

Introduction ix
One: More Truth, More Success 1
Two: More Success, More Happiness 27
Three: The Power of the Future with SBE 45
Four: Using SBE 53
Five: Ideas That Will Help You Succeed 79
Six: Using SBE to Become a Better Person 89
Seven: Gaining More Peace 99
Eight: Sharing the Bounty 113
Final Comments 123
About the Author 127
Blank SBE Sheets 131

Introduction

CAN YOU AFFORD TO TAKE the time to read this book?

I believe you can. *Success by Emotions* introduces a new application of age-old principles that will enable you to increase your happiness, boost your self-esteem, and improve faster in every area of your life.

If you do not take the time to read this book, you will miss out on learning about Success by Emotions (SBE), a tool based on laws of nature that you can harness to accomplish twice as much per unit of time (minutes, hours, days, weeks, months, or years) spent—and have a happier time doing it. It is not as revolutionary as the discovery of the wheel, but it will feel equally remarkable once you start seeing the results in your own life.

If you want to accomplish more in the future, then I believe you will be wise to take the time to read this book now. If you want to become a better person, this book will help with that, too.

But, keep in mind that just reading the book will not be enough. I have introduced SBE to many people, and some have missed out on its power because they were not willing to do the hard work necessary to see results. For them, it was just another good idea they assumed they already knew about. Or, they brushed it off because they were "too busy" to learn something new that would enable them to reach their objectives in less than half the time.

I promise you, the effort will be worth it. You will not only do everything faster, but things will also be easier to do. And the biggest benefit you'll receive will be the happiness you'll experience during the journey.

I know this to be true, after using the tool for over fifty years and sharing it with many others who have seen it change their lives. SBE has enabled me to dramatically increase my income, rapidly gain financial independence, love myself as I am, love others as they are, achieve objectives that I would have never thought possible, improve my relationships, and become a far better person than I was before. And it has enabled me to have each of these growth journeys in an easy, rapid, and pleasant way. SBE has done this for many others as well, and I know it will work for you, too.

Throughout my five decades of experience as an accomplished salesman and businessman, my key to successful investing has been my ability to recognize when

INTRODUCTION

the normal "risk relationship" is heavily in the favor of my investors. As a result, my investors' returns were about twice the normal returns for similar investments. All investments have risk, and all offer rewards. In most cases, if the potential for reward is high, then the risk is also higher than normal. Conversely, if the potential for reward is low (like in a federally insured bank's savings account), then the level of risk is much lower than normal. If you can find an investment that offers a high reward (similar to or better than that offered by the stock market) with a level of risk below that of a bank savings account, this is a great investment. Warren Buffett, the best investor of our time, calls these types of investments "no-brainers."

SBE is, in my opinion, a no-brainer. The risk is that you might spend some time reading this short book and working through the four-step process that will make you feel better about yourself. If you do not reach your goal after using SBE, you will still be better off and will have lost nothing. Your risk is zero. But, in the near certainty that SBE does work for you, you will have achieved your goal—plus, the hours spent will have saved you weeks (if not months) of effort in the future. Achieving goals in half the time will make many impossible goals now possible.

Are you ready to invest in the beautiful life and unlimited potential that is waiting for you?

—Bob Raybould

ONE

More Truth, More Success

SUCCESS BY EMOTIONS (SBE) IS a tool for personal growth and rapidly gaining more happiness, and it is based on three laws of nature; these are absolute truths, and they never fail.

The first two natural laws upon which this tool is based are accepted by all. First, that we are each born unique, and during our lives, we gain our own set of truths and limiting false ideas. Second, that the more truth we have in our lives, the better our lives work.

Now, the third natural law may be new to you—and it holds the key to gaining more happiness and success in your life. This third law is that we can accumulate enough emotions to remove our limiting false ideas and replace them with more truth.

SBE integrates these three laws of nature to help you find more truth in your life and bring you more happiness and success in a way that is faster, easier, and more enjoyable than anything you've ever tried before.

> If you're like me, and you don't like to read—if you like to get to the nuggets of truth without going through all of the words—you can skip to chapter 4 and start using SBE right away. This tool is enormously powerful, but you do not need to read the whole book to gain its value; the real value will come as you use the tool.
>
> So, to get started now, think of a small goal in one area of your life where you want to gain more happiness and a more positive view of yourself. It should be something you know you can accomplish in a few days or weeks but just have not done yet. Then, read chapter 4 and start using SBE. After you've achieved your first goal and have experienced the power of SBE, you can then return to the beginning of the book to deepen your understanding of the tool and learn how to achieve bigger goals—and do it faster and more easily. Enjoy!

Each of us were born perfect and complete. We were born with the innate ability to feel contentment and peace, and we were inherently able to give and receive love. We were born with the unique DNA, talents, abilities, and potential we needed to succeed. But, as we grew older, our experiences caused us to accumulate false ideas about ourselves.

In my case, I was born into a situation that provided me with unique advantages and unique disadvantages. As my life played out, all these combined and I learned a unique set of beliefs. Some of these beliefs were true and helped me move forward, and some were false—and these false beliefs kept me from seeing who I truly was; that I was born with all the abilities and talents I needed to be happy and succeed. I was still that person, but my false ideas were keeping me from seeing who I really was.

I had dyslexia and spent two years in the second grade. My father's experience in World War I left him with mental problems that he treated with alcohol. My mother's life was difficult and caused her to not feel or show emotions. Our family finances were relatively good, but also unstable. All these and other factors caused me to gain many false ideas about myself.

I struggled in school, but I found a way to succeed. I had both failures and successes, but my determination kept me moving forward in life. As the years passed, I faced more challenges, and the false ideas that I had accumulated caused me to go in circles instead of solving them. Then (as I will explain later), in my late twenties, I had a big failure. But, with persistence, I kept trying to succeed.

Up to that point, my life had been made up of a constant series of successes and failures, and my life looked like this:

SUCCESS BY EMOTIONS

Then, at the suggestion of a book I was reading to help me succeed, I listened to a recording called "The Strangest Secret" by the radio speaker and author, Earl Nightingale. Recorded in 1953, it was first given as a presentation to a group of salesmen and is now available on YouTube. The main message is that our thoughts shape who we become. (Many of Nightingale's examples are male-oriented, but women can gain value from the recording as well, if they can overlook this fact.) I listened to the recording repeatedly, and it opened my mind to thinking differently; I began to see that I could change my life by changing my thoughts. I also realized that I had more ability than I was showing in my actions, and if I didn't change my thoughts and actions, I would remain stuck—as I was and where I was. Before listening to "The Strangest Secret," I had been addicted to thinking and acting like a person who failed often. But, after listening to it many times, I came to believe that, if I could learn to think differently, I could also more easily act differently and change my results.

This new realization led me to discover a self-improvement method which I called Success by Emotions, or SBE. By using SBE, I was able to gain true ideas to replace my false ideas concerning myself as a businessman.

As a result, I went on to success after success in business. From then on, my life in business looked like this:

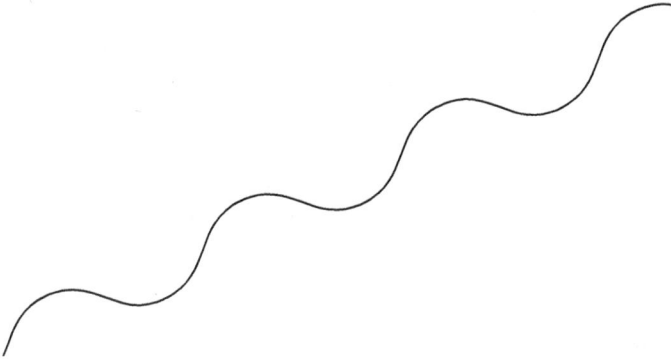

These two lines tell part of my story. The second line (after using SBE to achieve success) is about half as long as the first line (when I was still struggling before discovering SBE). Not only did I succeed, but I did it in about half the time it would have taken if I had continued to use traditional methods for growth and change. In addition, my journey forward was much more happy and joyful.

SBE is an entirely different approach from traditional methods of self-improvement. With traditional methods, we fight through the lies and false ideas we have accumulated. With SBE, we eliminate the false ideas *before* we begin the journey. In addition, because SBE enables us to free ourselves from our false ideas before we begin—when we are rested and fresh—the process is much easier and faster. If, in the process of learning to use SBE, you also spend two to three hours listening to "The Strangest Secret," the combination of the two will save you days, weeks, and even years of effort in the future.

SBE is such a different approach, and I never would have discovered it without first repeatedly listening to "The Strangest Secret." I am grateful that Earl Nightingale was able to share his special insights with us. I have simply added to his wonderful guidance with the process of feeling emotions. The recording not only taught me the additional truths I needed to learn before I could succeed; it also helped me overcome my addiction to thinking like someone who often failed.

Because I know firsthand the profound impact of listening to "The Strangest Secret" along with using SBE, I recommend that you start there. By listening to the recording a few times, you will come to know that you can shape your success by changing the way you think about yourself. I have introduced SBE to many people, but those who first repeatedly listened to the recording have been the most successful in using this tool.

A Brief Overview of Success by Emotions

Success by Emotions (SBE) is a tool that has been of enormous help to me. If you choose to use it, your life will improve far beyond your expectations.

With SBE, you will learn to accumulate enough positive emotions to expose your negative false ideas about yourself. Once you know they are false, your mind will eliminate them. The more false ideas you remove, the more you will reconnect with your true self and see yourself as the winner you were when you were born. You will then do whatever it takes to reach your goals. Because you will have replaced your false ideas with truth, you will find it easy to act like this person would act and create the results this person would create. Going through this process will also enable you to better serve and love others. As you do this, you will also love yourself more. These are the greatest gifts of using SBE because you will bring benefits to yourself and to others. It is all about love. More love will make your journey full of joy and happiness.

I discovered SBE in 1968, when I was on the verge of a huge failure. I was so desperate that I was willing to try anything. In doing that, I discovered this amazing tool.

At the age of thirty-two, I was married to a wonderful woman, had two wonderful children, and had served successfully in the United States Army in Germany for two years. I had just resigned from a position with a large corporation in New York, and I was returning to Salt Lake City, Utah, to sell life insurance. I had been an insurance salesman three years earlier, and at that time, I had not been successful. I had given up and had used my MBA to gain the job in New York. This time, I was desperate to succeed.

But, instead of succeeding, I was doing as I had been doing three years earlier. I was going forward and backward, not making any real progress. I was having ups and downs, and I was stuck at the same low level of personal acceptance.

Then, I discovered SBE, and my business life changed. In the process of applying SBE to my work, I went on to incredible success and my feelings about myself greatly improved. I still had struggles and setbacks along the way, but I was able to quickly overcome them and continue to move forward.

When I first discovered SBE, I attempted to share it with others because I was so amazed by the change it had made in my life. Fast-forward more than five decades, and I am still committed to sharing the power of SBE, which is why I have spent the last four years drafting this book, so I could share this tool with anyone who is willing to use it.

SBE will challenge you to think differently about yourself and see yourself in a new way. It takes courage to do something different and new. Thinking differently is hard (if not impossible) unless we first have a desire and prepare ourselves to do so. A strong desire may be enough for some. But it was not enough for me. I needed to repeatedly listen to "The Strangest Secret" to prepare myself for the process of using SBE.

Many of us are comfortable with the way we are, even if we want to do more or be more. We shy away from change because it can feel overwhelming. But SBE is entirely different from anything you have used to change. The beauty of SBE is that it doesn't require you to change who you are; you already have everything you need to succeed, you just need to reconnect with that truth. And, when you do, it becomes easy—and even enjoyable—to think differently, act differently, and change your life for the better. And listening to "The Strangest Secret" will help you overcome your habits of thinking the way you now think, so that you can be ready to use SBE.

Rather than listening to the recording, you may be able to jump in and start using SBE right away, but I have seen time and again that those who have achieved the greatest results from using SBE started by learning additional truth from the recording and changing their habit of thinking in their old, negative ways.

Throughout the rest of this chapter, I will explain how SBE works. Then, with that understanding, you can decide if you want to try the rapid approach, or if you want to take time and first listen to "The Strangest Secret." The latter approach will take longer, but if you take the time to listen to the recording, I can almost guarantee that you will have greater success using SBE.

Why Is Change So Difficult?

We all fight against growth and change, even when we know that it will benefit us. So what keeps us stuck?

1. **We're taught to conform.** As we go to school and live our lives, we are taught to follow the rules and learn the proper ways to behave. We are taught that conformity is the path to success. But, as my son has taught me, any idea taken too far can cause problems. We also develop a strong desire to conform our lives to the way

we are currently thinking. We want to stay the way we are, and we become almost addicted to thinking the way we have always thought. But this limits our creativity. A wise man once told me years ago that "if nothing changes, everything remains the same." Conforming keeps everything from changing. But we know that more truth will make our lives better, and using SBE requires that we let go of our false ideas and replace them with truth. This requires change.

2. **We fear the unknown.** What will our lives be like after we change? We can't predict the future, but what we do know is that life does not stand still. We can either continue to gain more false ideas, or we can change our lives and accumulate more truth. Using SBE can provide peace of mind in knowing that, although our lives will be different afterward, they will also be better.

3. **Our false ideas are powerful.** The limiting beliefs we've accumulated have been in control for a long time. Sometimes, it can even seem like they've defined who we are. But the truth is that we are so much more than that, and our false ideas can only continue to exist as long as we believe in them. In using SBE, we eliminate those false ideas and gain more control, which makes it much easier to succeed.

4. **We don't have time.** Many of us think we don't have time to make changes or go after our goals.

But that is not a valid excuse. Using SBE saves months (and, in some cases, years) of time by enabling us to reach our goals faster than anything we've tried before. Yes, it will take time to read this book and apply its principles. But those few hours spent will save so much more time in the long run.

So, while there are many reasons why it can feel hard to make changes in your life, the happiness and success you'll gain from using SBE will be well worth the effort. Achieving your first goal will feel the hardest because you will not only be removing the false ideas that are keeping you from your goal, but you will also be overcoming the false ideas that are telling you not to change. Trust in the process; SBE will make it fun and easy to reach your goals. And having a happy journey along the way will be your greatest reward.

Gaining More Truth with SBE

As I mentioned earlier, we were born with everything we needed to succeed. We had many inborn talents and abilities (we still have them; this is who we really are).

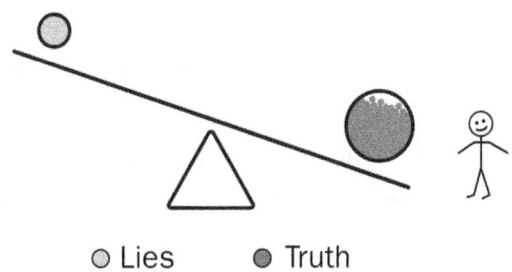

SUCCESS BY EMOTIONS

As babies, and soon afterward, it was easy for us to succeed. Without great struggle, we learned to eat, walk, talk, and run. It was easy for us to develop our talents and abilities.

But then life happened. We had different experiences. During some of these experiences, we gained false ideas about ourselves and became disconnected from our innate abilities. For example, at age three, we all could paint beautifully; we just naturally accessed the potential we were born with. Many years later, after accumulating judgments and expectations about ourselves, we've become convinced that only a lucky few are "talented enough" to paint beautifully; we've overlooked the natural potential we had accessed so easily when we were children.

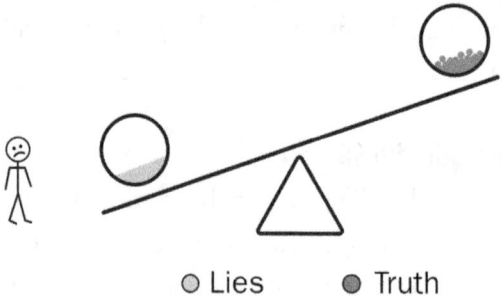

○ Lies   ● Truth

These false ideas tell us that we can't do things we have the ability to do. They slow our progress, and in some cases, even stop it altogether.

We use SBE to eliminate these false ideas by accumulating positive emotions that lead us to our true selves. By doing this, we are able to see ourselves more accurately. We again see that we have the ability to succeed. This flips the scale away from our lies and false ideas, and toward the truth about who we are. And when we think more positively about ourselves, that changes how we act and what results we create.

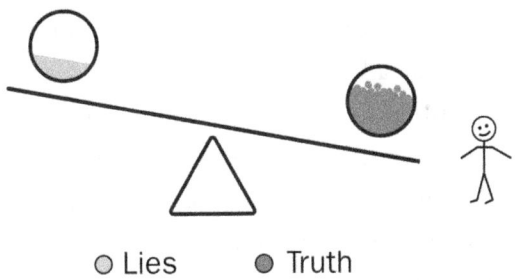

SBE works because it is centered around absolute truths, and it never fails. As Dr. Russell M. Nelson, one of the early pioneers of open-heart surgery, explains in his book, *Heart of the Matter: What 100 Years of Living Have Taught Me*:

> There are absolute truths, and there are relative truths. Relative truths often change as science and discovery produce knowledge heretofore unknown. Relative truths can also change as a result of personal opinion. But absolute truths never change. Gravity is an absolute truth. Gravity never varies. [...] Absolute truths are completely reliable, even incontrovertible. They do not change. This means that procedures and practices based on divine laws will work every time.

SUCCESS BY EMOTIONS

The laws of nature always work. And, the more we follow them, the better things work. Gravity always works. Planes with the proper engineering are always lifted up when they reach the necessary speed.

When Dr. Nelson was in medical school, doctors believed that, if anyone touched a human heart, it would stop. In time, they found that they could touch a heart, and it would continue beating. Then, they found they could handle a heart, and it would still continue to beat. They eventually developed a heart-lung machine so they could remove the heart from the body and the patient would continue to live. They later found that, if they altered the sodium-potassium ratio in the heart, it would stop beating, which would enable them to perform intricate operations that would be impossible to do while the heart was moving. Then, they discovered that, when they washed the potassium out with normal blood, the heart would start beating again. The more practice they had, the more they refined how they used this law of nature. But their refinements did not change the law; the surgeons just changed their understanding of the details that made the law work. Each new discovery allowed them to progress forward in doing heart surgery, and these pioneers found that this law of nature will always work.

The more truth we have about these laws of nature, the better our lives work. And, the more we use these laws, the more they can help us move forward. The laws do not change, but our new understanding of them enables us to more easily change our lives for the better.

MORE TRUTH, MORE SUCCESS

About sixty years ago, David C. Evans (the father of my good friend, David F. Evans), woke his son in the middle of the night to tell him that he had just put the first dot on a computer screen. He had discovered how to use another law. From that first dot, we now have all the marvelous smartphones and computer graphics we have today.

Each new discovery of truth opens the door for additional discoveries. Some discoveries are made after years of research. Others, like the apple falling on Sir Issac Newton's head, happen by chance. All these discoveries are made by brilliant scientists who have spent hours learning and experimenting. I am far from being a great scientist. As you will learn later, it was by pure accident that I discovered the natural laws that make SBE work. I simply sat down in a new car, and it made me feel different.

When I read these words in Dr. Nelson's book, a light bulb went on for me:

> "Surely," I thought, "there must be laws, or truths, that govern the beating heart." If we could discover those laws and then "obey" them, the results would be positive. It was the very idea that absolute truths, or divine laws, exist—and that following them would produce desirable results—that gave me new hope about discovering ways to repair a defective heart.

I realized that SBE works based on three absolute truths. The more I could understand SBE, the more I could use those truths to help myself and others move forward in their lives. SBE works—and will always work—because it is based on laws of nature. If we accumulate enough emotions, we will expose our unique false ideas, and our lives will improve. This will always be true.

As the years pass, we acquire relative truths about ourselves. They keep us from seeing the absolute truths about who we are. In using SBE, we regain those absolute truths; this changes the way we see ourselves and helps us change the way we perform and the results we accomplish. We gain a better view of who we are and what we can accomplish. Then, when our minds see that our old beliefs have been exposed as false, our minds now always treat those beliefs differently. The true ideas that replaced them are now in control, and the false beliefs are released. The longer we have held a false belief, the more emotions are keeping it in place. This means we need more emotions to expose it as false. But the natural laws that are working remain the same.

As studies are done on these principles, we will gain a clearer understanding of how these natural laws work. But, in the meantime, these laws will continue to work, and you can utilize their power with SBE.

Testimonial

"I was initially skeptical when Bob first introduced me to Success by Emotions. I approached the process with openness and a desire to believe that it could help me, but in the back of my mind, I wondered, 'What are the odds that this little book will help me?'

"I had read so many self-help books over the years, and I'd recently become increasingly obsessed with self-improvement, and yet, I was still stuck. I felt like I was spinning my wheels and getting nowhere. I understood the concepts of manifestation, visualization, belief, and mindset, but I couldn't flip that switch to change my limiting beliefs about myself. I was making little steps of progress here and there, and I found encouragement and insight in many of the books I was reading. But I knew I was still missing something. I was always looking for the next book, the next breakthrough, the next solution, unknowingly reaffirming to myself that I wasn't enough, that I needed some external knowledge and force to fix me. I felt lost.

"I had blocks that were keeping me from flowing. I've always been drawn to the analogy of a river. It flows effortlessly; it doesn't need help, it doesn't need anyone to get in there and push the water downstream. I've always wanted my life to flow like a river, and yet I felt the need to continually push when my flow was dammed up. I was fruitlessly trying to push through my life without first removing the blocks—the limiting beliefs, the fallen logs and debris of negative experiences and emotions that I'd allowed into my being. I was denying my natural state of flowing with ease. Like so many people, I was allowing past experiences, pains, failures, and rejections to define me. I knew this conceptually, but I still tried to push because it was all I knew how to do.

"By using SBE and switching my focus to really feeling how I wanted to be and how I would feel when I achieved my goals, those blocks have naturally begun to dissolve and break apart. All that focus I was giving to my problems was only reinforcing those blockages and damming up my river. By not giving them attention—and instead focusing on the positive, good feelings I wanted to feel and the happy, confident person I wanted to be—I've begun to taste the freedom that comes with being in my natural state of flow and ease. I now approach problems with curiosity, knowing there's always something to learn and new ways in which to grow.

"By practicing this method and focusing on the positive emotions, all the knowledge I've accumulated that at one point seemed only theoretical is now alive and real. I still find myself reflecting on this and thinking, 'This is too easy. There's no way it's this easy.' And yet, I can't deny the results. I feel different. Opportunities are coming into my life in new, unexpected ways. I'm not saying my life is now magically perfect. I still have problems, but I've changed the way I view them, and I find myself smiling and simply enjoying life rather than being weighed down by worry and stress. I'm excited to continue using SBE and experience the freedom that comes from making real changes in how I perceive myself and the world around me."

—Nate Myers

SBE Is a Process

I will walk you through each of the four steps to use SBE in chapter 4, but I'd like to start here by giving you an overview of what you can expect when going through the process.

First, you will set a goal and a completion date. You'll then list a few benefits you (and others in your life) will receive in reaching your goal, and a few emotions you will be feeling in the days, weeks, or months after reaching that goal and attaining those benefits.

You will then accumulate enough of the emotions you will be feeling after you have achieved your goal (i.e., after your completion date) to outweigh the emotions that are holding your false ideas in place.

Once your false ideas have been outweighed, they will be exposed as false. And when your incredible mind sees they are false, it will quickly eliminate and permanently discard them. With those false ideas gone, it will be very easy for you to achieve your goal.

Your First Step

I will now ask you to spend two to three hours and prepare yourself to use SBE by listening to "The Strangest Secret" a few times. As you will see, the main messages of "The Strangest Secret" are the following:
1. You have far more ability than you can possibly imagine.
2. You become what you think about.
3. Thinking in the same way will hold you back.

4. Conforming—acting like everyone else, without knowing where you're going or why—will make change difficult.
5. To change your results and actions, you need to change your thinking.
6. Goals will help you to think differently.
7. Seeing yourself doing what you will be doing after reaching your goal will help you act differently.
8. This will also help you start moving forward.
9. The easiest way to change your actions is to first change how you think.
10. Seek outside help and motivation.
11. Think good thoughts about yourself.
12. Use the thirty-day test to keep yourself moving forward.
13. You are rewarded in life for rendering service to others.
14. Worry about rendering more service, and the rewards will follow.
15. Rather than competing, it is easier to be more creative.
16. Keep on keeping on.

Remember, you're not required to do this first step before using SBE, but I know that it will give you your best chance at success. I believe in choices. The more choices we have, the better decisions we make. But our false ideas limit our choices. Some tell us we cannot do things we have the ability to do. Others tell us we do not want to do things that are in our best interest to do.

MORE TRUTH, MORE SUCCESS

The more false ideas we accumulate, the less choices we have. The more we remove those false ideas through SBE, the more choices we have. In addition, and even more importantly, the more *truth* we have. The more truth we have in our lives, the better they work.

You can choose to listen to "The Strangest Secret" right now, and keep listening to it as you read this book. Or, you can take a chance and see if using SBE on its own will be enough to allow you to achieve your goal.

We are all different, and many of us have no desire to put in the work to make any changes. Preparing to use SBE is a commitment, and not everyone will be willing to make that effort. Even though it is based on natural laws that always work, and I am promising that using SBE can save you years of time in the future, for some, the reward will not feel like it is worth the time. Keep in mind that there are over seven hundred hours in a month and over eight thousand hours in a year. Spending two to three hours to guarantee your success in saving months or years of time is a good return for that extra time. The biggest risk you face is missing the opportunity to find a tool as effective as SBE at increasing the quality of your life.

It is like taking a test in college. If you take the time to prepare before you take the test, your chance of success will be very high. But, if you fail to attend class and do not study for the test, your chance of success will be very low. If you take the time to listen to the recording, I am confident you will succeed in using SBE. Those two or three hours will save you years in the future. If your desire to succeed is not strong enough to spend that time improving who you are, then SBE is probably not for you.

> **Testimonial**
>
> "I am thrilled to share my profound experience with Bob Raybould's groundbreaking theories on using emotions to transform your life. Success by Emotions, which involves imagining a better future and allowing oneself to emotionally dwell in that envisioned state, has been incredibly powerful in my own life.
>
> "By employing Bob's method, I have witnessed remarkable changes. The process of identifying and removing the false, limiting thoughts that naturally hinder our ability to dream has been liberating. It has allowed me to see a brighter future with clarity and hope. As I embraced this envisioned future emotionally, I found myself gradually accepting this new reality on a deep, emotional level.
>
> "This emotional acceptance of a brighter future has had a transformative impact on my life. It has enabled me to become the person I always was, buried beneath layers of doubt and limiting beliefs. Bob Raybould's theories have truly empowered me to embrace a new reality and to experience life with renewed purpose and joy.
>
> "I wholeheartedly recommend SBE to anyone seeking profound and lasting change in their lives. Bob's insights and techniques are not only powerful but also life-changing."
>
> —Jared Bauer

In the beginning, almost everyone will face the same hurdle when attempting to use SBE. Many of us have a lot of false ideas that will tell us not to use SBE because it involves using emotions. Over the course of our lives, we have been taught to be logical and to be careful with our emotions, which can cloud our judgment, make us vulnerable, and lead to potentially dangerous mistakes. Instead, we learned to pride ourselves on being dependable, reliable, consistent, and trustworthy. At first, we might fear that using our emotions will interfere with our ability to uphold these qualities. But, in reality, having more truth in our lives will help us with all of these qualities—and SBE is a powerful way to gain more truth.

Emotions are like gasoline, dynamite, electricity, or fire. They can be used to create valuable results, and they can be used to create harmful results. Emotions enable you to use SBE and create value in your life. In the beginning, your emotions will attempt to keep you from using SBE, because they are still tied to your limiting false beliefs. Your emotions will make the process seem scary and dangerous. While this can be a frustrating dilemma, you can view it simply as a terrific demonstration of the power of your emotions. Your emotions are what you will be fighting against as you begin to use SBE. And they are also the factor that makes SBE so powerful and so beneficial.

Emotions are neither good nor bad; they are just emotions. The meaning we place on them is dependent on what we do with them. Love, anger, fear, hate, and all other emotions can either help us move forward or they can hold us back. Take fear, for example. If you were to find yourself in a burning building, fear would compel you to run to safety. This is a true and beneficial use of this emotion. On the other hand, fear may be keeping you from trying SBE because a false idea has convinced you that you are destined to fail. This is a detrimental use of this emotion, and it is holding you back from achieving your goals. In both cases, the emotion in play is fear, but each scenario has a very different result. Truth helps you move forward, and false ideas hold you back. SBE is a way to help your mind expose false ideas and let them go.

Listening to "The Strangest Secret" six to eight times may be enough to help you overcome whatever emotions are holding you back. Rereading this section will also help.

Why Is SBE So Powerful?

There are two reasons for this. The first has to do with our incredible minds. We are all wired in a way that causes us to act in harmony with the way we currently see ourselves. We do not act in harmony with who we are. We do not act in harmony with the DNA we were born with. We do not act in harmony with our talents and abilities. Instead, we act in harmony with our current view of ourselves. That view is formed by our experiences and by accepting the false ideas that have been passed on to us by our parents and others.

When our false ideas are still in place, we view ourselves as someone who will have trouble succeeding, or someone who is going to fail. To keep us acting in harmony with the way we see ourselves, our minds make sure that is what happens. In addition, because we are all connected to one another, our minds work to keep others from helping us.

When we go through SBE and see ourselves as someone who will succeed—or someone who has already succeeded—the above factors are reversed. Now, our minds are helping us succeed. In my experience, we also create a new, successful version of ourselves that is gently but firmly pulling us toward our goal. Our minds also reach out and gain the help of others. This makes succeeding much easier and much more pleasant.

The second and biggest reason SBE works is because it strengthens our connection to the world around us, whether that's with our friends and loved ones, our communities, or even the kindness of strangers. Tapping into this rich interconnectedness is only possible when we view ourselves as being worthy of receiving its rewards. If our false ideas have convinced us that we cannot succeed, then we block ourselves from forces that can help us. If we reverse this, then our interconnectedness can come to our aid, and once we have this assistance, we can accomplish any objective we were born with the ability to do.

SBE only allows us to remove our false ideas in one area of our lives at a time. But, in time, we can remove more false ideas and achieve more of our objectives. Knowing that we can succeed once we have gained this outside assistance makes it much easier for us to keep accumulating emotions throughout the SBE process.

We were each born with different talents and abilities, and as we use SBE, we will each succeed in our own unique way. Because I believe the following, I feel that SBE can be of value to everyone:

- We all have more abilities and talents than we are using.
- We all have false ideas that are holding us back.
- We can all gain more help from our incredible minds.
- We can all gain more help from the world around us.
- We can all experience success more rapidly.
- We can all have more happiness in our journeys forward.

I hope that you will give SBE a chance to improve your life.

TWO

More Success, More Happiness

SUCCESS BY EMOTIONS (SBE) IS a tool that can make your journey through life easier and happier. As I explained in the previous chapter, I discovered SBE after I had failed at selling life insurance, and it enabled me to succeed at an aggressive goal and then continue to succeed beyond my expectations.

Over the years, I've shared this tool with others who have experienced the changes firsthand. (You'll read testimonials from some of them throughout this book.) I taught it to my iPhone salesperson, who was struggling to get an internship. He went on to get five offers and several other incredible accomplishments in just a few months. My grandson was struggling with anxiety, and I shared SBE with him. He still has small bouts of anxiety, but he rapidly succeeded at two jobs and is now successful in business for himself. The tool has assisted all three of us—and many others—to move forward professionally and to become better people. It will enable you to move forward in all areas of your life, too.

You will accomplish goals and objectives in a fraction of the time it would take you if you were using traditional growth methods. More importantly, SBE will help you love yourself and others more, and your journey toward success will be more enjoyable. And, once you achieve your first goal, you will go on in that area of your life to achieve goals beyond your wildest expectations.

SBE: A New Approach to Growth

SBE is a process of growth that is different from traditional growth in a number of ways.

In traditional growth, we do the work and gain the results we desire. This new success changes the way we see ourselves. I call this approach DO, RESULTS, BE.

In comparison, SBE is based on three undeniable laws of nature. With SBE, the majority of the work of changing the way we see ourselves and feel about ourselves is begun and completed before we begin to take any physical action working toward our goals. I call this approach BE, DO, RESULTS. How does this work? Our minds act in harmony with the way we see ourselves. By first changing the way we see ourselves (BE), we enable our minds to help us act differently (DO) to achieve our goals (RESULTS). Our minds are incredibly powerful. Having them helping us (rather than fighting against us) makes an enormous difference.

A good example of traditional growth is given in Dr. Amy Cuddy's TED Talk presentation, "Your Body Language May Shape Who You Are," which you can watch on YouTube. There are many different types of traditional growth. The type Dr. Cuddy used was the "fake it till you make it" approach. In her example, she followed the DO, RESULTS, BE model.

In her presentation, Dr. Cuddy explains how an accident had convinced her that she was far less than she once was. Her self-view was reduced. Before her accident, she had seen herself as a successful person. She had felt confident that she would succeed. In her mind, if the accident had not happened, she would have easily gone on to great success. But, when the accident happened, it changed the way she saw herself. For a time, she saw herself as someone who would not succeed.

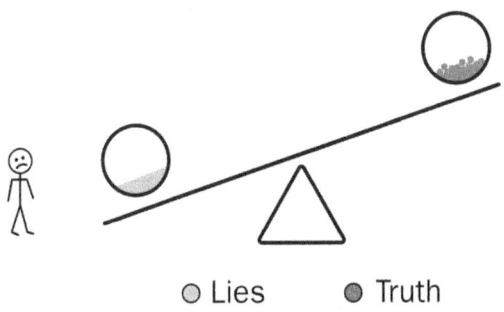

○ Lies   ● Truth

Then, she was able to use the "fake it till you make it" approach to overcome and push aside the false ideas that had been created by her accident, and she went on to have great success.

SUCCESS BY EMOTIONS

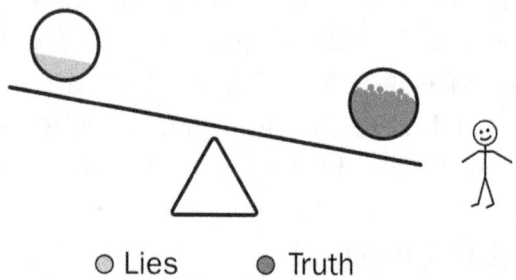

○ Lies   ● Truth

But, even after achieving significant success, she still felt like an imposter. During that period of time, deep down, a part of her still felt like the person who was not able to achieve success. It took her a couple more years to see herself as a success.

I have my own story of following a traditional path to growth. I did not experience an accident, like in Dr. Cuddy's story. Rather, I have dyslexia, and it caused me to spend two years in the second grade. In addition to my dyslexia (as I will outline in more detail later in the book), my situation at the time of my birth resulted in several experiences that severely lowered my self-view. This all caused me to believe that I was dumb. For many years, I saw myself as a dumb person.

But I was able to use traditional growth methods to fight through my false ideas and change my behaviors, even while I still thought of myself as being dumb. After a long time of doing this, I finally improved in my schoolwork, and I no longer believed that I was dumb. However, this process took many years, and I did not feel that I was really smart until I started working for a large corporation in New York. They only hired engineers from the top one-third of their classes. When I took a test they gave to those engineers, my score on the test put me in the top 5 percent of engineers who had graduated in the top one-third of their classes. And this helped me go from feeling that I was dumb to learning that I was smart and good at solving complex problems.

And, while I did ultimately achieve my goal, the process could have been much faster and more enjoyable if I had used the SBE system back then.

What Makes SBE Different?

Success by Emotions is very different from traditional growth. In SBE, the first step is to change the way we see ourselves. Instead of DO, RESULTS, BE, the order in SBE is BE, DO, RESULTS. We first use SBE to see ourselves as the person we will be after we have achieved our goal. This enables us to more happily take action toward achieving our goals. Achieving our goals is then simply an expression of who we are.

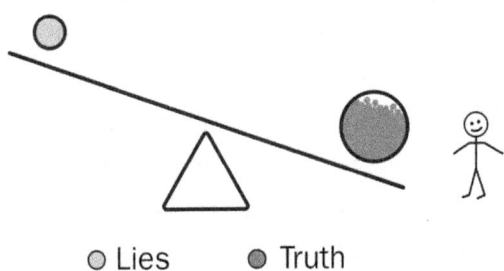

○ Lies ● Truth

SUCCESS BY EMOTIONS

I discovered this in 1968. Prior to that, in 1964, I had received my MBA from the University of Utah. Rather than take a job with a large corporation, I decided to be my own boss and sell life insurance. After fifteen months of working sixty-five hours a week and not making much progress, I quit. I decided I was not cut out to be a life insurance salesman. Instead, I used my MBA to obtain a job with the corporation in New York. It was there where I took the engineering test that convinced me I really was smart.

During my two and a half years with that corporation, I read everything I could to help me succeed in selling. I wanted to be a successful life insurance salesman and be my own boss. I had already failed once at this, and I was trying to get enough information to enable me to succeed on my second try. When I had finally built up enough confidence to return to selling life insurance, I left New York and moved back to Salt Lake City in 1968.

As I mentioned in chapter 1, it was at this time when I began listening regularly to "The Strangest Secret" by Earl Nightingale. Following the directions given in the recording, I set a goal to significantly increase the annual income I had been earning in New York, and to do so within two years.

The recording was perfect. It did not ask me to see myself as a successful insurance salesperson. I had already tried and failed at doing that. I had no idea what my being a successful insurance salesman would look like.

Instead, the recording prompted me to picture myself doing what I would do *after* I had reached my goal. Doing this would help me think differently about myself.

My goal was to quadruple my income. Driving a Porsche was what I would be doing after I had reached my goal. So I went to the nearest car dealership and sat in the driver's seat of a Porsche 911 coupe. As I sat down and wrapped my hands around the steering wheel, I discovered SBE.

A surge of excitement, gratitude, and happiness coursed through me. I was feeling how I would feel while driving my own Porsche 911 after I've reached my goal. I began to *feel* like a person who drives a Porsche.

These emotions took me by surprise, and I savored them for a good, long while. A salesman came over and asked me if I would like to go for a test-drive. I said no. I just wanted to sit there and feel those wonderful feelings.

Those feelings opened the door in my mind and allowed me to see myself differently. I was filled with a new level of truth about myself. I didn't know it at the time, but I was experiencing new laws of nature in my own life. I was beginning to feel like a successful person. I was now ready to change the order and create a method of self-improvement that would be totally different from traditional growth; I was ready to become a success *before* I started working toward my goal. BE, DO, RESULTS would be my path forward.

Listening to "The Strangest Secret" opened my heart and mind. It taught me that, if I can change my

SUCCESS BY EMOTIONS

thoughts, I can change my actions. That gave me hope. But it did not change the way I felt about myself. My false ideas had still controlled me at that time. When I had previously set my goal, I'd changed the way I was *thinking*. But, when I sat in the Porsche, I was changing the way I was *feeling*. This change enabled me to accumulate enough positive emotions to outweigh the negative emotions that had been holding my false ideas in place. This had been impossible for me to do when I was using traditional methods of growth and relying on intellectual arguments.

Before I sat down in the Porsche, my self-view as an unsuccessful person had been firmly in place. I had the ability to succeed, but my emotions were holding my self-view in place and telling me I could not succeed. That was a lie. If I continued to believe that lie, success would have remained beyond my grasp. My faulty self-view, not my truth, would have remained totally in control.

But, by sitting in the Porsche, I had expanded that idea. I began to accumulate the feelings I would be experiencing *after* I had reached my goal. Sitting in that car and feeling those feelings for ten or fifteen minutes was enough to cause me to gain enough truth to believe that I could succeed. I was feeling the emotions I'd feel in the months after achieving my goal; I was feeling like a successful person, like someone who drove a Porsche. Absolutely nothing in my life had changed; I was still struggling to succeed. But I was beginning to feel how I would feel after I had succeeded. I was not yet convinced that I would succeed, but I believed that I was capable of succeeding. I had made the initial flip of the scale in my mind.

Now, over fifty-five years later, I understand what was happening to me at that time. I was beginning to discover and understand these new natural laws. Those new feelings started to change the way I saw myself. They began to expose my false ideas as imposters. I had the ability to succeed; I had always had the ability to succeed. But my false ideas had been keeping me from seeing that truth. The more of these emotions I accumulated, the more I exposed my false ideas. My mind then eliminated those false ideas—and I saw my true self. I had already accomplished enough in my life that I did not see myself as a loser. But my false ideas had been keeping me from seeing how much of a winner I am.

"The Strangest Secret" and other methods of traditional growth also probably work based on natural laws. If you spend enough time seeing yourself doing what you will be doing after you have reached your goal, your motivation will eventually reach the point at which you can effectively fight through the false ideas that are holding you back. That is how different types of traditional growth work; our false ideas have power over us, and we need to gain additional personal power to fight through them.

SBE uses a different natural law. It does not make you any more powerful or give you more strength, determination, or persistence to fight through your false ideas.

Instead, it is based on the law that if you accumulate enough emotions to outweigh and expose your false ideas *before* you do any work toward your goal, you will not need any additional personal power to fight through your blocks because they will already have been removed.

Until you understand this difference, you will keep trying to make SBE the same as the other growth methods you have used in the past. But it is different. I get it; we have all moved forward at one point in our lives by using traditional growth. These methods have probably helped you achieve some goals in the past. But why wouldn't you choose the path that is easier, faster, and more enjoyable?

Almost all of us have had experiences that have reduced our self-esteem and introduced false ideas into our lives. Almost all of us have accepted false ideas from others, and we've added those to our accumulation of false ideas that have reduced our self-view. We are all winners, and the more truth we gain, the more we will see that fact.

These false ideas only exist as long as we believe them. Once we expose them as false, we will cease to believe them. Once we stop believing them, they will fade away and lose their power over us.

Leveling the Playing Field

Another key difference between SBE and traditional methods of growth is that SBE makes success available to everyone. You might find yourself doubting whether this tool will work for you. Maybe you've come to believe that only someone with a successful background, high self-esteem, a large amount of self-discipline and self-determination, or great willpower and persistence can create a successful life.

Well, when it comes to using traditional methods of growth, there might be a select few who are strong enough to succeed by fighting through their false ideas.

But SBE changes everything. With SBE, everyone can experience a faster, more enjoyable path to success. It takes a much lower level of self-discipline, persistence, determination, and willpower to use SBE and accumulate enough emotions to eliminate your false ideas and gain more truth.

With SBE, everyone can be successful. The playing field is much more level than it ever has been. We can all gain more truth in our lives easily and rapidly.

Testimonial

"When Bob Raybould first told me about Success by Emotions, I was intrigued. I had tried countless self-improvement techniques in the past and had experienced some growth, but it always felt like a long and arduous journey.

"SBE is completely different because the process of accumulating emotions is pleasant and exciting. As I envision having already achieved my goal, I feel myself being uplifted and empowered by the positive emotions I've attached to that accomplishment. This sets me up to engage more fully with each day's tasks, and it energizes me to give more of myself in learning, growing, and connecting with others.

"I've also come to some significant realizations about myself while releasing my false ideas. For example, using SBE helped me recognize that I had been holding on to the notion that having a successful business meant that I would have to sacrifice my family life and personal well-being. It turns out that I had picked up this false idea from a few business coaches I had followed, as well as from some of my fellow entrepreneurs, who glamorized the 'never-ending hustle' of running a business. I was able to release this false idea by replacing it with positive emotions such as feeling peaceful, joyful, and grateful. This has shifted how I approach my work, and how I connect with my clients and customers.

"I am so thankful to Bob for sharing SBE with me. It is such a valuable tool, and it has helped me create a more gratifying and abundant life."

—Anna Krusinski

Emotions Are Stronger than Logic

My fifty-plus years of success as a salesman has taught me that most sales, and most important decisions, are made at the emotional level and are then justified with logic. In my personal experience, trying to overcome emotions with logic is like trying to put out a fire with a squirt gun. On the other hand, working to overcome even long-held negative emotions with strong positive emotions gives us a great chance of success.

Our past experiences have created beliefs and conclusions that have been stored inside us for a long time and have combined to form the self-view of someone who cannot succeed. This false view has been held in place by our negative emotions.

If we want to change this conclusion—and our current self-view—we need to use our emotions.

When I first came across SBE, sitting in that Porsche created enough good strong emotions to flip the scale and begin to free me from my negative emotions and false ideas. From then on, every time I touched the steering wheel of my Volkswagen Beetle, I felt like I was touching the wheel of that Porsche. Each time I did this, I added more units of emotion to the side of truth.

At that time, I did not understand anything about SBE. I was simply recreating the experience that had taken place when I had sat in the Porsche. I did not realize it at the time, but I was accumulating emotions. All I knew was that doing this felt great. I did not see that I was on my way to success. I had no idea that I had discovered new laws of nature. On some days, I was still filled with doubts. In addition, I could not figure out how I was going to succeed. But I remained consistent and kept accumulating more units of emotion.

Three weeks after I first sat in the Porsche, the biggest change took place. I had been fighting against my doubts all day, and I had gone home feeling discouraged. During the night, the emotions I had been accumulating flipped the scale in an enormous way. As I slept, my mind absolutely concluded that I would succeed. When I woke up, I saw myself as someone who would succeed.

I had no clue how I would succeed, but I *knew* that I would. My new self-view was firmly in place. I was a big-time winner, and I finally knew it. It had taken me three weeks to accumulate enough emotions to totally convince myself that I would succeed.

Now that I knew I would succeed, nothing else mattered. I knew that I was a success, and I knew I would achieve my goal. I would happily do whatever it took; I would work as hard as I needed to work. Once I felt this way, my mind had no choice but to help me, and I also started to receive help from others around me. It was only a matter of time until I succeeded.

I had not changed as a person. I did not have any new DNA. I was the very same person I had been four years earlier when I had gotten so discouraged that I had given up and taken an easier job.

What was the difference? It was this: I had quit believing the lies I had been telling myself. I was the same person, but I had replaced many of my false ideas with truth.

The fact that I knew I would succeed helped me learn the new skills I needed to succeed. It also helped refine my abilities and my talents. I was still working about sixty-five hours a week, but I was having fun. And I did ultimately reach my goal.

Testimonial

"I love self-help books! No matter the topic, I am nearly always the target audience. When it comes to prosperity and success, I have come a long way from being in psychiatric hospitals in my teens and experiencing chronic depression and anxiety in my twenties and thirties. But, despite years of various types of therapy and multiple twelve-step programs, I still felt listless and 'held back' in life. I desperately searched for some other self-help program that could magically fix the rut I was in. However, I didn't realize that what was holding me back was my own false belief system.

"Success by Emotions has opened me up to a whole world of possibilities. Being asked to think about and meditate on how I will feel after I achieve my goal has put a whole new—but very logical—spin on things for me. Listening to 'The Strangest Secret' a handful of times also helped put SBE in perspective.

"The goal I chose to try was financial stability. Well, in the few short months I have been practicing feeling my future-success feelings, I have more than doubled my income. I also had a blissful aha moment when I realized that life isn't about taking on more work, meeting impossible deadlines, and accomplishing unrealistic goals, but about surrendering to what life is really like at any moment in time.

"While Bob recommended I spend forty minutes to an hour each day in meditative contemplation, I instead meditated on my positive feelings for several minutes frequently throughout my day, releasing my false emotions in the process. Somehow, SBE was helping me to have hope that financial prosperity would come. It was helping me to think differently about money and success in a way that no twelve-step program or decades of therapy had ever done for me.

"While these positive shifts were beginning to happen, I had a brief period of doubt about SBE. Then I realized that I had skipped a crucial step: I needed something tangible to represent my goal. What I didn't realize until later was that this was my scale-tipping point. This was when I was so sure of my success that I knew I would reach my goal, no matter what. Right then, I used some of my surplus funds (something I'd never had before SBE), and purchased tickets for a trip to California, my home state. Having that tangible ticket in hand was the breakthrough I needed for SBE to take hold.

"I was at the stage of being willing to do whatever it took. I had a few setbacks, but instead of sinking into total panic and fear, I was already feeling the emotions and confidence of financial success. Sure enough, an offer came along for a high-paying job that was much more fun and exciting and would require far less time and effort, which meant I would be able to stay solvent without having to work so many hours.

"SBE has changed my thinking … and my life. I am obsessed with this process! I can't wait to use SBE on a new goal! It works. It really does!"

—Leya Booth

Overcoming the Doubt

As I have been using SBE over the last fifty-five years, this sequence has been consistent. Just before I accumulate enough emotions to know that I will succeed, my false ideas put up a last-ditch effort to stay in control. It is like they are real voices that do not want to be removed. I am filled with doubts and discouragement, and I am tempted to give up.

In these situations, I just trust that SBE will work, because I know that natural laws always work. I keep accumulating emotions. Not long after I show my commitment to continue accumulating emotions, SBE works, and I am even more confident of my future success.

Over the years, the doubts have come up again and again. And the stronger the feelings that were holding me back, the bigger the step forward I have taken in my self-view and confidence when I've finally accumulated enough positive emotions.

In traditional growth methods, our false ideas fight to stay alive during the whole journey. In my experience, when using a traditional approach, many of my false ideas stayed alive even after I had experienced success and moved forward. Instead of removing them, I had just found a way around them.

With SBE, we remove the false ideas before we begin the journey. For this reason, our false ideas may not recognize that they are at risk of being eliminated until those final few days or hours. This has repeatedly been my experience.

THREE

The Power of the Future with SBE

ONE OF THE INCREDIBLE ADVANTAGES of using Success by Emotions is that our growth can continue endlessly after we achieve our first goal. Once our lies and false ideas are removed, they stay removed—and our future goals become easier to achieve.

About two years after I first sat in that Porsche, I was driving my very own Porsche, and I was living in a new home. After another two months, I had quadrupled my earnings.

At that time, I did not set another goal, but I continued to accumulate emotions. My income continued to double each year for the next four years. Then, just twelve years after I had discovered SBE, I was financially independent.

Our growth becomes limitless with SBE because, in addition to removing our false ideas, we are also seeing ourselves in a more positive, empowered light. And, because we are programmed to act in harmony with the way we see ourselves, we act differently and create the results we desire.

The Long-Lasting Power of SBE

SBE has been an important part of my life for over fifty-five years. It has enabled me to accomplish so many goals I could not have accomplished previously. The time I have saved using SBE has created time for me to do things I would have never otherwise had time to do. SBE has saved me *years*.

As you use SBE, you will find that it will become easier to achieve your goal each time. Because of this, I suggest that you start (in chapter 4) with a small goal and work your way up to bigger goals.

When I first discovered SBE, I was able to increase my income fourfold. If I had gone for a higher, more aggressive goal, I am not confident that I would have been able to overcome the false ideas that were holding me back. In fact, my initial goal was to increase my income sixfold. A good friend told me at the time to reduce it to fourfold. I missed that goal by about two hundred dollars, but I have chosen to call that close enough.

After that, my circumstances continued to improve as I kept using SBE. I was presented with several new opportunities and was able to evolve from being just a great salesman to also becoming an excellent businessman.

THE POWER OF THE FUTURE WITH SBE

In addition to gaining assistance from my own mind by using SBE, what was happening in our country at that time was almost perfectly suited to help me gain great success. In setting my goal to quadruple my income, I must have somehow known what opportunities were just around the corner. I gained a significant advantage by becoming one of the first financial planners in the Intermountain West, and I helped form one of the first tax-sheltered real estate firms in the United States. But, without SBE, I would not have been so confident and would not have progressed so rapidly.

This happened about five years before everyone else figured out the current tax laws. When this happened, everyone tried to buy real estate, and we sold all of our real estate because prices were so high. Two years later, the new tax laws reduced the value of real estate by about 25 percent. This series of unexpected events greatly assisted in my incredible success. But SBE allowed me to continue with success after success in the following years.

My income continued to double each year over the next four years. This meant that my income doubled six times in six and a half years.

These numbers demonstrate the point I am attempting to make. The initial flipping of the scale takes dedication. But the benefits that follow that dedication far exceed anything we can even think about at the time while we are working to flip the scale toward truth.

The initial increase in my earnings was a 400 percent increase. But, because of the false ideas I had removed, the happiness I was feeling, and the truth I had gained about what I was capable of, my income continued to double again and again. The first increase—although it was the hardest to achieve—was a small fraction of the total increase.

Without experiencing it for yourself, it is hard to understand the significant improvement you will be making after you achieve your first goal.

Keep in mind that each person's level of success will be different. It is rare to be a great salesman. It is also rare to be a great businessman. But it is even more unusual to be both a great salesman *and* a great businessman. I am very lucky to have achieved both traits. This is an important fact to remember. The average person reading this will not have the same level of business success that I have had. Not everyone will become rich, but we all have different areas in which we desire to excel, and SBE can help us achieve those goals. SBE does not give us power over circumstances that are beyond our control, but it does enable us to remove our false ideas and become better people by gaining more truth in our lives. Everyone using SBE can eliminate enough false ideas to be successful enough to live comfortably. Once we have that much, working to become better people becomes a better use of our time than trying to accumulate more and more wealth. Your success will look different from mine, but you will still experience the joy in the process, you'll know more of your true self, and you'll find success more easily each time you use SBE.

THE POWER OF THE FUTURE WITH SBE

My wife once read a book written by Gary Emery, PhD, a psychiatrist who has worked with the top movie stars. In the book, he commented that we all have strengths and weaknesses. He found that the movie stars who were at the top of their profession also had many weaknesses. He concluded that, if we could see everyone's strengths and weaknesses, we would see that we all are about average people. I would agree. Almost everything mechanical or electrical I have tried to fix has ended up worse than when I began. I not only can't fix it, but I make it worse. For example, I worked for several days installing a new part on a car but ended up with three or four leftover parts that I did not know what to do with. Even though we are all about average, I still believe that everyone who uses SBE will not only succeed, but that their initial success will open the door to other successes beyond their current expectations.

That is a very bold claim. The following testimonial supports that claim.

Testimonial

"Success by Emotions has been a transformative force in my life, guiding me through incredible personal and professional milestones. Before discovering SBE, I was like many others—caught in a cycle of limited successes and frustrating setbacks. I knew I had potential, but I couldn't quite harness it.

"Everything changed when I embraced the principles of SBE. By eliminating the false ideas and emotional barriers that had been holding me back, I found clarity and confidence in my abilities. This shift in mindset was pivotal; it didn't just help me achieve my goals—it made the journey to success enjoyable and fulfilling.

"As a result, I experienced an unprecedented increase in my income, effectively doubling it within a short period. This newfound financial freedom allowed me to pursue my long-held dream of starting an investment company. The principles of SBE didn't just stop at getting me started; they provided the continuous motivation and emotional resilience I needed to navigate the complexities of the investment world.

"Today, I'm proud to manage over 100 million dollars' worth of real estate. This is a testament to the power of SBE. The method's unique approach to removing false ideas and fostering a positive, determined mindset has been integral to my success. It's not just about achieving financial milestones; it's about the holistic improvement of my life. I am happier, more confident, and more successful than I ever imagined.

"For anyone feeling stuck, overwhelmed, or simply wanting to elevate their life, I wholeheartedly recommend SBE. It has transformed my life beyond my wildest dreams, and I believe it can do the same for you."

—Sam Froerer

In experiencing the long-term benefits of using SBE, you will also find that your journey becomes smoother. Life can be likened to riding a bicycle. If we keep moving forward, it is easier for us to keep our balance. The slower we go, the harder it is to keep our balance. This is a good description of what happens when you use SBE. Throughout your life, you had accumulated so many false ideas that the hill you were riding up was very steep. You may have even lost your balance and given up on your goals. But, by using SBE, you first accumulate enough emotions to remove your false ideas. And, with the false ideas removed, the hill becomes very gentle. It may still have a few steep parts, but your momentum will be so strong when you reach these that going over them will be pleasant and you will be able to maintain your balance. Achieving your goals will become fun and easy.

FOUR

Using SBE

WHEN I FIRST BEGAN DRAFTING this book, I was hoping just to write a booklet. I wanted to provide others with a quick fix for finding happiness and improved results. I had no idea I had discovered natural laws, absolute truths, that would make change and growth easier. But, as I gained a deeper understanding of the power of Success by Emotions, I knew it needed to be a long-term process. In this chapter, I'll cover the ins and outs of the four steps of this process.

Remember, the benefits come after challenging work. In traditional growth, the hard work happens during the journey. But, with SBE, the hard work happens mostly in the beginning as you accumulate emotions and eliminate the majority of your false ideas. That hard work will bring you benefits far beyond your expectations.

SUCCESS BY EMOTIONS

Choosing Your Goal

I am now going to ask you to choose a goal for your first time using SBE. The goal you choose is not nearly as important as the fact that you are beginning to use SBE. But, the more emotional drive behind your goal, the easier it will be to accumulate your emotions.

In chapter 1, I asked you to prepare yourself to use SBE by listening to Earl Nightingale's "The Strangest Secret" multiple times. In this chapter, you will now be given the opportunity to use SBE to eliminate the false ideas that are holding you back.

To succeed, you will first need to set a reasonable goal. It should focus on one area of your life where you want to feel more happiness, and it should be something you know you can accomplish within a few days or weeks. You can still think big in terms of your long-term goals, but when you're just getting started, I suggest you select something small to focus on first. As my mentor used to tell me, "Survey large fields and cultivate small crops."

When I first discovered SBE, I was desperate to succeed, and I chose a very large goal. In hindsight, I also recognize that, at that time, part of me thought that what Earl Nightingale was suggesting in "The Strangest Secret" was too good to be true. And, back then, I loved being right, to the point that I was willing to fail just so I could prove that what the recording was saying was too good to be true. You may have some of the same feelings about what I am writing here. Thankfully, a good friend helped me change my goal and settle on one I could achieve.

Years later, in 2004 when I was working with the University of Utah football team to help them use SBE, I learned from my past mistake and started small in working with just a few players. I had success with this small group. The coach, Urban Meyer, asked me to work with six of his players in the offseason. I worked with them in depth using SBE and had them listen to "The Strangest Secret." The team went on to a high final ranking and an undefeated season, and four of the six players I worked with went on to play in the NFL (one decided football was not for him, and the other remained a significant contributor to the team). The credit goes foremost to the team and the coaches, but I do feel I was a small part of their success.

In setting your own goal, remember that the bigger the goal, the more feelings you will need to accumulate. Because of this, I suggest you choose a goal that is important but can be attained in a few days or weeks. Spend some time thinking about it, but not too much time. It does not need to be a perfect goal. SBE gives you a tool to achieve one reasonable goal after another. Once you have achieved your first goal, the door will be open for much additional success. The key is to choose a goal that will help you succeed.

Below are a few testimonials from people who have used SBE on small goals. The first was written by someone who has successfully used SBE on a goal that had eluded him for a long time. The second one comes from someone who has been working on his goals for years but only started writing them down when he tried using SBE—and he finally started seeing results. The last testimonial is by someone who has been working on his goals with SBE for over a year and has kept moving forward.

> **Testimonial**
>
> *My friend, Erik Groszyk, played college basketball in the Ivy League and has been using SBE on small, short-term goals.*
>
> "Early in our friendship, Bob Raybould had described Success by Emotions. I've always enjoyed discussing SBE with him because certain aspects of it correspond to certain 'discoveries' I've made in my own life over the years. Since I was a teenager, I have practiced positive thinking and visualization. While these techniques have helped me find success and happiness in life, my conversations with Bob clarified areas where my beliefs about myself and my goals could be further refined.
>
> "Bob extended a small suggestion to me: that I pick a small goal to begin experimenting with his theory of SBE. The goal that has deepened my understanding of SBE the most was the desire to make ten consecutive free throws on the basketball court. This is something I did so regularly as a young person, I hardly thought much of it at the time. However, as I

now play basketball less often, it is something I rarely accomplish anymore. A free throw is a very simple shot—you are stationary (as opposed to moving quickly), you are lined up perfectly straight just fifteen feet from the basket, and there is no defender to rush you or alter your shot. However, all these factors can actually lead even the most experienced professional to overthink their shot. Historically, even the greatest shooters will make this shot about 90 percent of the time, while even good shooters by professional standards might make this shot just 70 to 80 percent of the time in games. The poorest shooters will make it less than 50 percent of the time (worse than a coin toss).

"I could not remember the last time I had made ten free throws in a row, even though I'd tried most of the times that I went to the gym. It was not because of lack of ability, but there was some mental block preventing me from achieving the delicate balance of focus and relaxation sometimes called 'flow state.' I thought this would be perfect for testing Bob's theory of SBE.

"Within a couple days of doing SBE, I could simply access the emotions in my mind and allow them to permeate my body. Previously, during my shooting practices, I would visualize the ball going through the net; this was a habit I had developed as a teenager. Only through working with SBE did I realize that this technique had been incomplete. I could imagine the outcome of a successful free throw attempt—the ball cleanly falling through the net—but still have the emotional experience (anxiety) of missing a shot. In this way, the image I was visualizing was in conflict with the emotions I hoped to achieve, and SBE clarified this discordance for me. In fact, I realized that visualizing the ball going through the rim was actually less important than experiencing the satisfaction and joy that this outcome would provide to me.

"Bob had told me many times that the key to SBE was to actually experience the emotions of achieving your goal in a visceral way, but I had not thought to replace other aspects of my visualization with simply experiencing emotions. As far as identifying the benefits of accomplishing my goal, I believe this had a clarifying effect in my mind. It forced me to think more about *why* I desired a certain outcome, which served to further convince me of its personal importance, and it also helped me contextualize my goal as an intermediate step in my larger journey as an athlete. This helped reconcile a dichotomy that relates to our goals: we are trying to accomplish something that challenges us now, but will seem very simple to the future version of ourselves. (And, in this particular case, it was previously easy to a *past* version of myself.)

"A week after beginning SBE, I successfully made ten free throws in a row with seemingly little difficulty. I could not remember how many years it had been since I'd done this, and it felt like an enormous triumph—not over some vaunted opponent, but over my own biased, counterproductive thinking. When I did it again a few days later, it felt so casual that I hardly thought about it. By this point, my mind no longer treated it as some insurmountable task, but as an inevitable outcome. The anxiety and mental chatter I had previously experienced—especially after making seven, eight, or nine shots in a row—had mostly dissipated. Success, as they say, became a habit for me in this small regard. This entire experience has helped further clarify the power of the mind, and it's led me to wonder ... what other tricks is my mind playing on me?"

—Erik Groszyk

Testimonial

I have shared SBE with John Lund, and he has received value from simply writing down his goals on his SBE sheet.

"I have had the pleasure of knowing Bob Raybould for more than twenty years. Bob has been an important mentor in my life, both personally and in business. I feel fortunate that Bob has shared with me his progress regarding the power of positive thinking, and I have benefited from his advice.

"Bob asked me to follow very specific directions to put his Success by Emotions concept to the test. This task required me to write down a single goal that I was confident that I have the natural ability to accomplish and could achieve within a few weeks.

"My first thought regarding this task was simple; I certainly don't need to write this goal down on paper! This is a goal that I think about every minute of every day of my life! Why write it on paper? I was happy, however, to do this for Bob, as he is a dear friend and mentor.

"I pulled out a sheet of paper and began to write my goal. I was amazed at the emotion I felt as I did this! Writing my goal with ink and paper took my goal to a whole new level emotionally. *Wow!* I had never felt these emotions like I did when I committed them to writing! I felt these emotions as if my goal were already accomplished!

"Although this entire experience lasted only a few minutes, it was profound and touched me to my core. The difference? Committing this simple goal to writing made it absolutely real to me.

"I *never* would have guessed that using pen and paper would make such an enormous difference. I look forward to repeating this valuable exercise with more important and longer-term goals. Thank you, Bob!"

—John Lund

Testimonial

Andy Robertson is a business associate whom I have known for several years. As he recounts below, he has been enjoying the long-term, cumulative benefits of using SBE regularly.

"I'm truly overwhelmed with my results from Success by Emotions, especially given how little time and effort it requires.

"After much hemming and hawing, I finally drafted a list of goals that had already been bouncing around my head for some time. They were not new, as I had been thinking about them for many years. I then made time to quietly review my list every morning before my day got busy.

"Within a few short days, I'm here to tell you that I had surprisingly strong feelings of confidence, determination, and happiness. From a logical perspective, it makes sense to me that the concept of repeatedly focusing on something will keep it top of mind. However, I wasn't prepared for the clarity of positive emotions inside my head and heart. It was empowering. And I was in awe.

"In the beginning, these feelings weren't there if I didn't look at my list. Now that it's been a year of using SBE, I can unlock the same empowering feelings when I mentally slow down for a few moments and focus on how I'll feel when achieving my goals. These feelings fade without intentional action on my part, so my challenge is to regularly make time to do the work. All of this has reinforced that SBE works for me—and I sincerely hope that it will work for you."

—Andy Robertson

Four Steps to Success

Although using SBE requires time and commitment, the process consists of just four simple steps. As you go through these steps, the main work you'll be doing will be to accumulate more of the positive emotions you will be feeling in the days, weeks, or months after you have achieved your goal.

Before we dive into the specifics of how to complete the four steps, here is a quick overview of the process:

1. You will first accumulate enough emotions to begin to *believe* that you can succeed.
2. As you accumulate more of these warm emotions, you will *convince yourself* that you can succeed.
3. Then, as you accumulate even more of these same emotions, you will eliminate enough false ideas to the point that you'll *know* you will succeed. At this point, you will also start to receive assistance from your incredible mind and your interconnectedness with the world around you.
4. Finally, once you know you have all of this assistance, you will *become obsessed* with succeeding at your goal. Knowing that you will succeed, it will become easy for you to do whatever it will take, and you will continue receiving even more assistance. Your false ideas will have been replaced with truth, and you can now do anything you have the talent and ability to do.

Actions trigger feelings, and I felt this firsthand when I discovered SBE by sitting in the Porsche I dreamed of one day owning. Each time I touched the steering wheel of my Volkswagen Beetle, I felt how it would feel to touch the steering wheel of my very own Porsche. When I imagined myself sitting in the Porsche, I was in a different place doing something different. Ever since then, whenever I've set a goal, I have connected to the process of accumulating emotions by using a tactile cue with my hands. For example, I have pinched my SBE sheet, pinched a congratulatory note, or pinched something else that signified success, or I've lightly clenched my fists. I have done this over and over to train myself. Whenever I use these tactile cues, I feel all the emotions I will be feeling after I have achieved my objective.

I also incorporated a tactile cue when I was helping the University of Utah football team in 1984 by teaching them to use SBE. Their season was already underway and their coach, Chuck Stobart, saw that SBE would help the team, so he took a chance and asked me to talk to his players and teach them how to use this tool. I asked them to visualize what they would be doing in the few days after they had achieved their goal. The team decided they'd imagine themselves eating a celebratory dinner together. I then asked them to feel how they will be feeling at that dinner. To help them connect with those emotions, I had the idea to ask each player to carry the handle of a dinner knife in their pocket. (I did not want to give them sharp knives, so I went to a restaurant supply house and bought a hundred knives, and then I went to a knife sharpening shop and had them cut off the blades and smooth the ends of the remaining handles. The knife handles were now small enough to fit in a pocket.) By using SBE and connecting with their tactile cue, the team improved, and they were all happier in the process (even though they came short of their goal). For years afterward, whenever I would meet one of the players from that team, they would tell me that they still had that knife handle and were still using it to help them move forward in their lives.

You can increase the effectiveness of SBE by using a similar tactile cue to bring up the emotions you'd like to access and more deeply attune to the power of SBE. The more you do this small action, the more you will create the positive emotions, and the more you will be able to do what you need to do. This is your path to success.

Now, it's time to fill out your own SBE sheet. Use the blank sheet at the end of this chapter as a template, and refer to the sample sheet as an example. (You'll also find additional blank SBE sheets at the end of the book.)

On a sheet of paper, your phone, or a computer, write down these items:

- Your goal and completion date (give yourself a reasonable amount of time to accomplish this; for your first goal, it should be something you can accomplish within a few days or weeks)
- The tactile cue you will use to connect with the new emotions (I suggest pinching your SBE sheet)
- Two or three benefits you—and others in your life—will gain by reaching your goal
- Three or four emotions you will be feeling in the days, weeks, or months after you have reached your goal

USING SBE

Once you've completed your SBE sheet, it's time to go over the four steps of SBE in detail so you can follow them as you work toward achieving your first goal.

Step One

First, you will accumulate enough emotions to initially flip the scale. This will cause you to feel a positive change, and you will now *believe* you can succeed at your goal. But this does not yet eliminate your false ideas; that will happen during the next steps.

After this initial flip, you will just keep accumulating emotions. So, if you miss this initial feeling, it is not important. But I believe you will feel a little different and a little better as the scale is flipped.

To complete step one, slowly read your entire SBE sheet. Simply reading the words you have written will begin to accumulate emotions.

We are all different, but my experience tells me that going through the SBE sheet four or five times will be enough for you to obtain this different feeling. A bigger goal may take more repetitions.

If you are not sure whether you have reached that feeling, just keep accumulating those same emotions. The moment will arrive, and you will know it when you feel it. You will begin to see yourself as the winner you really are.

Step Two

In this step, as you continue to accumulate emotions, you will become *convinced* that you can succeed. You will also begin to eliminate your false ideas.

To complete step two, read your SBE sheet again. But, when you get to the benefits, read the first one. Then, re-read each emotion. Do the same with each benefit. Each time you read an emotion, attempt to experience it more deeply.

In addition, each time you read a benefit, visualize how it will feel to have more of that benefit in your life. The more you connect your emotions to the benefits you and others will be receiving after you've reached your goal, the faster and easier it will be to accumulate emotions.

The feeling you are attempting to experience is a good, pleasant feeling; a feeling of increased confidence.

While you're working on step two, you might find it helpful to listen to certain types of music that can change the way you feel. (Being dyslexic, I could not listen to music while I studied, and music does not help me accumulate emotions. But we are all different.) Music helps many accumulate emotions more rapidly. It can change the way you feel and can open your heart.

You can also sit in one spot during step one and then move to another spot when completing step two; this signals to your brain that you are shifting the way you're thinking. It will remind you that the emotions you are feeling are the ones you will be feeling after you have achieved your goal.

Step Three

In this third step, as you continue to accumulate emotions, you will eliminate enough false ideas to the point that you will *know* that you will succeed. On large goals, this will take time and dedication. But the minutes and hours spent doing this will save you months, weeks, and even years in the future.

Once you have accumulated enough emotions to know that you will succeed, you will begin to receive assistance from your mind and from others around you. I know when I am to this point because I am sure I will succeed, but I am not sure how I will make it happen. Soon after, the answers start coming, as well as help from many sources.

To complete step three, continue repeating the process in step two until you feel differently. This will indicate that you are beginning to see and feel the real you. You will likely feel good inside, or a little better, more pleasant, noticeably happier, more confident, or more energetic.

(In my experience, this is the step that has been most difficult because it is at this point when I briefly feel some doubt. To help me push through, I remind myself that I now have assistance from my incredible mind and other sources to help me succeed. With this in mind, I keep accumulating emotions and eventually reach step four.)

Step Four

Then, after you have accumulated even more emotions and have remained open to receiving support from your mind and other sources, your energy and enthusiasm will increase to the point where you will become *obsessed* with achieving your goal, and you will fully enjoy the journey forward. It will be only a matter of time until you succeed. Knowing this, you will be able to easily do whatever it takes to succeed.

To complete step four, you will need to do two things. First, you'll need to start doing the work—and keep doing whatever it takes—until you achieve your goal. Second, you will need to continue accumulating emotions and gaining more truth. This will remove additional false ideas, help maintain your confidence, and allow you to keep learning how to better succeed and have the courage to keep moving forward.

In the beginning—and even after you become effective at using SBE—it may not be clear when you have moved from one step to the next. That is just fine. You'll just need to keep accumulating emotions during all four steps and during your entire journey toward your goal. The most significant change you will notice in every goal you work toward will be how happy you are during the journey. That has been the number one benefit for me and others who are successfully using SBE.

Give It Time

After you take the time to listen to "The Strangest Secret," set your first goal, and accumulate enough emotions to be confident of your future success, you still have more work to do. But it will be fun and pleasant work, especially once you understand the learning curve of SBE.

When you first start using SBE, you may find that your progress feels slow or flat. This is because it will take time for you to process the emotions you are accumulating and remove the false ideas that have been controlling you. The most difficult part of using SBE is having faith in the process and just continuing to accumulate more units of emotions. At times, it will seem like nothing is happening; but, if you keep doing it a little longer, and then even a little longer, it will happen. These are natural laws, and they will always work. It takes time, but the extra minutes (and even hours) spent will save you days, weeks, and months in the future.

As you continue the process, something miraculous will happen: you will start thinking and acting like a successful person, you'll acquire new skills, and you'll further develop some of your inborn talents and abilities. You will also make some mistakes during this time—and that's okay. This is the perfect time to make mistakes, because the risk is low, and you can learn from those mistakes (see chapter 5) without creating enormous damage.

Be patient with yourself during this time. Eventually, as you keep using SBE, you will grow faster, and your rate of success will skyrocket, as shown in the chart below. Reminding yourself of this visual can help you to enjoy the process of accumulating emotions.

SUCCESS BY EMOTIONS

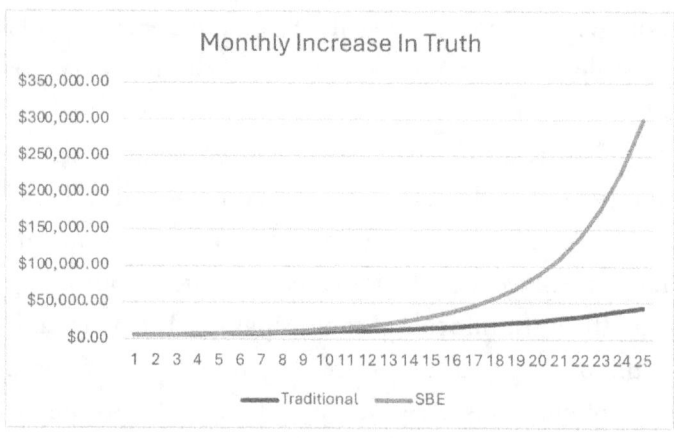

In this learning curve, your first goal will occur within the first part of the line. Most of your success will come *after* you have achieved that first goal. So, for now, set an attainable, reasonable goal you know you can achieve. And keep in mind that, even with a small and achievable goal, you will go through that initial period of lower production and accomplishment. Eventually, with the lies and false ideas gone you will succeed far beyond your initial expectations; it will just take some time to do it.

Everything we do is a process, and SBE is no exception. We are always more successful when we prepare before we act, so it is necessary that you remain diligent with accumulating emotions and give the process time to unfold in the proper order.

When learning to drive we first become a good driver and then we drive fast, after we've developed our skill through practice. If we were to drive fast before becoming a good driver, the probability of an accident would be very high. Similarly, when one is learning to play a musical instrument, it is important to learn to play before giving any type of performance. If one were to try to perform before they had learned to play the instrument, it would not turn out well. The same is true in sports. Those who play in teams take time to prepare so they will not let down their other team members. They do not go on the field until they have taken many necessary steps to prepare. In all things in life, we need to take the steps in their proper order.

This is a big reason traditional growth is such a slow, hard, and frustrating process—because, in these methods, we attempt to move forward without taking the time to first remove the false ideas, gain more truth about ourselves, and change the way we see ourselves; we're not proceeding in the correct order.

Instead, with SBE, we first remove our false ideas, gain the necessary truth about ourselves, and change the way we see ourselves; this process creates a foundation for the exponential growth you saw in the graph. And the journey itself is easier and shorter!

Decisions, Decisions ...

SBE can also been a great help in making decisions by enabling you to feel how you will feel in the days *after* you have made the correct decision. Once you have accumulated enough positive emotions toward this goal, your thinking will become clearer and the decision will present itself to you.

Before I discovered SBE, I had trouble making decisions. It got so bad at one time in my life that I worked out a system I thought would help me make decisions better and faster. I just said to myself, "In this case, what decision would this particular friend make?" I would figure out what decision that friend would make, and then I would make that decision. I had such a low opinion of myself and believed that I could not make a good decision, but if I thought about what a good decision-maker would do, I knew the answer.

This turned out to be a broken system because I actually had the ability all along; I just lacked the confidence to trust myself. So I trusted what I thought my friend would decide. I was just tricking myself into making good, rapid decisions.

Once I started using SBE to help me think and act like a successful person, I was able to rapidly make great decisions on my own.

A Few More Tips

As you continue to move forward, it might be helpful to make note of the false ideas that are eliminated. Many we do not notice, and they just fade away; but some we do notice as they are eliminated.

I still remember when I eliminated a major false idea as I was first discovering SBE. About the time when I was coming to believe I would succeed, I was sitting in my car waiting for the light to change. Then, a thought suddenly popped up in my mind that told me I could never be successful.

My mind then flashed back to being with my father when I was about ten years old. My father often took me to the farmers market. While we were there, he would point to someone and say, "He's rich, and he's a crook." We trust what our parents teach us, and I'd heard this enough times from my father that I accepted it as the truth. My young mind falsely concluded that, in order to be rich, I would have to be a crook. Years later, while sitting at that red light, I knew I had no chance to succeed because I was committed to integrity.

But I had initially flipped the scale by that point, and my mind was now helping me. It brought up memories of successful people who I knew were honest. At that moment, I recognized that my idea about needing to be dishonest to succeed was false, and I let go of it. It died as soon as I stopped believing in it.

You may also need to relisten to "The Strangest Secret" two or three times throughout the process. Earl Nightingale's guidance can be a powerful reminder that you have the power to change your life by changing the way you think—and by changing the way you *feel*. Every little thing you do to help yourself access more positive emotions will increase your chances of success.

Finally, as you follow the four steps of SBE, remember to stay connected with the world around you. Accumulating emotions through SBE will bring you to your truth, and as you gain more truth about yourself, your mind will gain new ideas and open you up to new opportunities. We are all connected, and others will come and help you succeed. The more you try to help others in the process, the faster the additional truth you need will seem to come to you. And, the more you focus on lifting and assisting others, the more truth you will gain to help you succeed.

Your next step is to continue to use SBE. It will make every other thing you do much easier. But it will not remove problems; they are there to help you learn lessons and grow. You will still face problems, but they will all be easier to deal with by the time you have finished this book. You will learn to view these problems as your friends that will help you be stronger, develop your talents, and learn new skills. The key to all of this is to keep accumulating emotions and gaining more truth.

There is a successful version of each of us. While we are accumulating emotions, we are reconnecting with this successful version of ourselves that is gently pulling us toward our goal.

Blank SBE Sheet

My Goal:

_____

_____

_____

Completion Date:

_____

Tactile Cue:

_____

> **REMEMBER ...**
> By continuing to accumulate more emotions, I am continuing to get a better view of my true self—and that person is gently pulling me forward.

BENEFITS:

1.

2.

3.

EMOTIONS:

1.

2.

3.

4.

Sample SBE Sheet

My Goal:

_____

Completion Date:

_____

Tactile Cue: Pinching this SBE sheet

_____

> **REMEMBER ...**
> By continuing to accumulate more emotions, I am continuing to get a better view of my true self—and that person is gently pulling me forward.

BENEFITS:

1. _____
2. _____
3. _____

Choose two or three of the following benefits, or others that are important to you:

- Learn to better use the natural laws of SBE.
- Gain more truth.
- Gain more help from my incredible mind.
- Gain more help from the world around me.
- Learn to see myself as a winner.
- Become more of who I have the potential to be.
- Gain more control in my life.
- Find more happiness in my life.

- Gain a greater level of peace in my life.
- Become more financially secure.
- Do something I need to do.
- Change something I want to change.
- Increase my faith in myself.
- Become a better person.
- Have more fun being who I am.
- Be more at peace with who I am.
- Find happiness and satisfaction in the journey.

EMOTIONS:

1. _____
2. _____
3. _____
4. _____

Choose three or four of the following emotions, or others that are meaningful to you:
- Gratitude
- Excitement
- Happiness
- Pride
- Confidence
- Satisfaction
- Peace
- Love
- Joy

FIVE

Ideas That Will Help You Succeed

AS YOU BEGIN TO USE Success by Emotions toward your goal, the following ideas will be helpful to you. (If you are still deciding on what goal you'd like to achieve, you can come back to this chapter and work on developing these habits and skills later.)

Thinking and Acting Like A Successful Person

Now that you have been introduced to SBE, I would like to introduce you to another skill. Used together, they will almost guarantee your success. But, far more importantly, they will guarantee you a happier, more peaceful journey on your way to success.

Successful people have developed the habit of finding a way to use everything that is happening to them as tools to help them become even more successful. This is why successful people do not quit, do not blame others or circumstances, and keep moving forward until they succeed. They are not bothered by mistakes, setbacks, failures, and difficult circumstances. They always end up learning lessons and eventually finding a way to succeed. They see these types of situations as friends placed along their path to help them learn valuable lessons.

Based on my own personal experience, going through the process of using SBE is helpful in forming the habit of thinking and acting like a successful person. When I first learned this habit, I had not yet used SBE. I'd acquired this habit as a separate undertaking, and it took me over six months to do. Now that I understand SBE better, I am suggesting you use a different approach.

With everything you've learned so far about SBE, you know that you are already a successful person. You just have some false ideas that are keeping you from seeing that fact. (And you're using SBE to release those false ideas.) When things go wrong, or when you are faced with a problem, take a moment to pause and remember that this experience is there for a reason. It is there to help you learn something that will help you be even more successful in the future. It may be to help you learn a new important lesson you need to learn, or it may be there to help you remove some false ideas that are keeping you from seeing that you are already a successful person.

SBE gives you a tool to rapidly learn these lessons. You do not need to fight through your false ideas to succeed. You can use SBE to accumulate enough units of emotions to gain the additional truth you need. For years, I have heard people say, "When the going gets tough, the tough get going." After discovering the power of SBE, I would now say, "When the going gets tough, it is time to stop, accumulate emotions, and remove the false ideas that are making the going so tough."

When you have a setback, just pause and say, "That is great," then find a way to learn something that will help you be even more successful in the future. Use SBE and feel how you will feel in the weeks or months *after* you have learned this lesson that your life is trying to teach you. As you do this, you will change the way you see yourself. Now your mind will help you gain new skills, improve your abilities, and refine your talents. Then, achieving your goal will be easier and faster, and the journey will be more fun and joyful.

Successful people are optimistic and happy. They are able to accomplish goals which initially seemed impossible. Once I began to see everything that was happening in my life as friends, there to help me learn lessons, my life was not only happier but also incredibly easier and more rewarding. The more this habit becomes a part of your life, the easier and more fun your life will become.

I have also learned to recognize the messages from my body in the same way. Feelings of sadness, despair, frustration, or discouragement are there to help me. They cause me to pause, slow down, and look more closely at what is actually going on. They are my friends. As I treat these feelings as friends and love them, they help me to learn important lessons.

SBE can also help you learn the lessons your body is sharing with you. For example, if you lack the motivation to accomplish something that is in your best interest, you can use SBE to gain additional truth and know that you were born successful enough to succeed and achieve your objective. This will increase your desire to act and move forward.

Forming these habits of thinking and acting like a successful person will help SBE become your default action to overcome unpleasant experiences. It will help you use those experiences as stepping stones toward your greater success.

My mentor was one of the smartest men I have ever known. Before retiring, he had been the head of the Federal Housing Administration, which meant he had been in charge of about 300,000 government employees. He often told me, "Take the time to contemplate, and when the inspiration comes, have the courage to act." When I would go to him with the business challenges I was facing, he would always give me the same advice: "See it through." I followed his advice, and it always seemed to work out. With the help of contemplation and SBE, I always found a way to learn lessons from the problems I faced.

I also have a good friend who is very successful. Like me, he has learned that, in business and in life, things are seldom smooth. He feels that the way to succeed is by learning to deal with our problems and finding successful ways to solve them.

These are two examples of people in my life who have taught me to think and act like successful people think and act. The more I do this in all areas of my life, the better things work out. When I cannot solve a problem, the very first thing I do now is pause and relax a little. Then, I use a combination of SBE, contemplation, and thinking like a successful person to move forward.

Testimonial

"Meeting Bob Raybould, and using Success by Emotions, has changed my life. I grew up on a ranch in rural New Mexico, and I eventually found my way to the University of Utah. At nineteen years old, I started working at Apple, and I was failing at balancing my job with my computer science studies. After undergoing a major jaw surgery, I faced more challenges but managed to secure a permanent part-time role at Apple. However, things took a downturn when I lost that job temporarily and struggled with my studies, leading my parents to suggest that I return to New Mexico. Fortunately, I got my job back and managed to complete my first year of studies while also completing an internship.

"One day, while working at Apple, I met Bob Raybould, who introduced me to 'The Strangest Secret' and SBE, which he said could help me achieve any goal. Initially skeptical, I eventually embraced Bob's advice and started setting goals, including securing an internship with Boston Consulting Group.

> "Though I faced rejections, including one from Apple for an engineering internship, I kept pushing forward. Bob's guidance helped me change my mindset, leading me to land an internship with Lockheed Martin, and a year later, a position with Boston Consulting Group.
>
> "Through Bob's mentorship, I have learned to view myself differently and pursue my goals with renewed confidence. Bob opened my eyes to my potential, helping me transform from feeling lost to achieving goals I had once thought were impossible. His teachings have been instrumental in shaping my journey and driving me toward a successful future. If *I* can do it, I can only imagine what someone else could accomplish, because I am an average person who now knows about the tool."
>
> —Ezekiel Jaramillo

Using SBE in the Face of Tragedy

Even after you've developed the ability to welcome life's challenges as lessons and opportunities for growth, you may still find yourself faced with especially difficult situations that feel insurmountable. When tragedy strikes (the loss of a loved one, a tough medical diagnosis, divorce, job loss, etc.), you may feel like you can never be happy again. But using SBE during these times can help you regain balance.

In times of tragedy and personal loss, we intellectually know that in the future we will again see things more accurately and see that we have many things to be grateful for. But, in those dark moments, everything can seem hopeless. When all seems lost, SBE can help us accumulate enough emotions to move us forward to our truth, to a place of happiness and well-being. Gratitude is a key emotion for doing this. However, while we will move through the same four steps of SBE, in cases like this, we also need to mourn our loss. If we just stuff those negative emotions and push past them, they cannot be exposed and eliminated. Depending on your situation, you may want to get outside help from a therapist to guide you through the mourning process while also using SBE to support your efforts.

A Method for Accumulating Emotions More Rapidly

In 1985, I had the privilege of working with Keith Henschen, PhD, who was on the staff of the University of Utah as their sports psychologist. Keith had helped the university's gymnastics team win their first NCAA championship, and many more thereafter. He was also a sports psychologist for the Utah Jazz. After discussing SBE with Keith, he felt that I was introducing a new type of visualization.

Keith believed that there were two skills which were fundamental to effective visualization. The first skill was that of concentration. The second skill was the capacity to rapidly move from one level of being and into our zone of high performance (the "zone").

To master the skill of concentration, he had his athletes look at a coin or their thumbnail and see how long they could concentrate on it without looking away. For those who did concentrate, they immediately and easily fought through their tension and "locked in." This took them less than a couple of seconds.

Most others could only maintain their concentration for about five or six seconds before losing focus and looking away. Keith pointed out that emotional tension was forcing them to lose their concentration. He had them try again and just fight through the emotional tension until they locked in. Once they knew what they were doing, almost all could fight through that tension and lock in in less than three or four seconds. He had them repeat this, and each time, stay locked in for a longer period of time.

Next, he taught his athletes the skill of rapidly transitioning into the zone. Interestingly, he had them first learn to move themselves into a state of relaxation. They learned to do this by getting into a comfortable position and then repeating a phrase, such as, «Whole body, comfortably warm," until they felt a relaxing sensation course through their bodies. (The first time I attempted this exercise, it took me approximately thirty or forty repetitions before I felt the sensation.)

He then told them to keep practicing this exercise until they could summon that same sensation with only three or four repetitions of the words. (This took me several sessions, and in each session, it took considerably fewer repetitions to achieve the relaxed sensation.)

I am now glad that I took the time to master these skills, because they have not only helped me in the past, but they now serve to assist me in rapidly accumulating emotions with SBE.

When I transitioned into the zone for the first time, I was surprised by how much faster this exercise enabled me to accumulate emotions. As I said to myself, "Mind and body in the zone," I knew I wanted to go into the zone for accumulating emotions. After three or four repetitions of those words, I felt a change in my body. Then, as I read the emotions on my SBE sheet, or thought of the emotions, I accumulated them much more rapidly.

Mastering these two skills has an extremely broad application. They will allow you to move to an area of high performance in any area of your life, and to do so rapidly.

SIX

Using SBE to Become a Better Person

I'D NOW LIKE TO SHARE with you an example of how I used Success by Emotions for a larger goal. A few years ago, I decided that I would use SBE for something more important than just improving my professional results. By this time, I had already learned that SBE was much more powerful than I had originally understood. So I decided to use the tool for a truly significant goal: to become a better person.

Becoming a Better Person

I knew that if I could be a better person, my life would work better. I had the ability to do it, but I did not yet have the desire to change. I planned to use SBE to gain enough truth about the benefits of becoming a better person so that I would want to make this change.

SUCCESS BY EMOTIONS

By becoming a better person, I would love my wife and family more. I would be less narcissistic. (At the time, I did not think that I was narcissistic, but a therapist had told my wife that I was. I assumed I at least leaned in this direction, because I loved to be in control and loved to be right; I was very competitive and had a lot of insecurities. Having less of these qualities would help me be a better person.) In addition, at this time in my life, I was always trying to be special and stand out from other people. As I will outline in the next chapter, SBE later enabled me to move away from needing to be special and toward being a normal person with strengths and weaknesses. I am sure part of my desire at that time to be special was because I wanted to be better than others. Now, in wanting to be a better person, I wanted to love myself and others as we are. My completion date for my goal was eighteen months away.

SBE in Action

To help convince myself of the truth that I could become a better person, I wrote myself a letter from my wife, congratulating me on having made significant progress toward becoming a better person. I wrote it on a piece of notepaper and placed it in one of the accompanying envelopes. As my tactile cue, I held the note and started accumulating the emotions I would feel in the weeks and months after I became a better person.

It took me about seven days to accumulate enough emotions to convince myself that I would succeed. Once

USING SBE TO BECOME A BETTER PERSON

this happened, I saw myself as a better person. (I thought this was quick progress, compared to the three weeks it had taken me to reach this step when I had used SBE over fifty years earlier.)

When I began, I did not *want* to become a better person, but I knew my life would work better if I made this change. I knew there were many areas of my life in which I could become better. But I did not want to change; I was happy with who I was, even though I was probably stuck. I was successful, and my value was coming from my successes and material objects, and not from who I was. This created a conflict for me. Intellectually, I knew I would be better off if I were a better person. But, emotionally, I did not want to do it.

Flipping the scale increased my desire to become a better person. And, as I added more emotions, I solved that internal conflict. I began to feel more of the values that would come to me as I became a better person. The more emotions I added, the more I wanted to add even more emotions. Now, the successful Bob I had created was gently pulling me toward being a better person. I was on my way toward becoming a better person, and I was having fun adding emotions and enjoying a happy journey on the way to my objective.

As I continued to use SBE toward my goal, negative memories of the past came up. At first, they bothered me. But, in time, I recognized that they were just pointing out mistakes that I had made when I had not treated others in a loving and kind way. And I could see that

SUCCESS BY EMOTIONS

I needed to gain more truth concerning a better way to treat others. To do this, I just needed to focus on accumulating emotions and leave the rest to the assistance I would receive from my incredible subconscious mind and the world around me. This has been a pattern that has continued as I have used SBE. This pattern has been so consistent that I am now learning to rejoice whenever something is bothering me, because it means I am about to learn a valuable new truth.

I kept accumulating emotions, and on my eighty-sixth birthday, I opened the congratulatory letter I had written. I still had a number of false ideas to overcome (as you will learn in chapter 7), but I was now feeling and acting like a better person in many ways. My original completion date has passed, and I knew I could still grow more toward becoming a better person. The false ideas stayed removed, and I continued to move forward. I began to feel more emotions that I'd previously blocked. The wall I had built to keep me protected from feeling and showing emotions was beginning to come down. Before, the pain of my early childhood experiences had been in charge, and I'd had no hope of ever moving beyond them. But now I suddenly found myself experiencing emotions and feeling more love in my life. I loved everyone around me. Feeling more love was wonderful, but it was a new experience, and I still had more to learn, so I used SBE to help me through this period of transition.

Enjoy the Journey

As you're using SBE to become happier and achieve success, remember that the goal is not so much about what you will accomplish, but about what kind of a person you will become in the process. You will succeed at both, but feeling whole, complete, content, and at peace will be the accomplishment that will bring you the most joy. Once you have flipped the scale and continued to accumulate emotions until you know you will succeed at your goal, the barriers will start to come down. You will start finding out who you are, and you will start realizing the power of the unique talents and abilities you were born with.

And, when you have reached your goal, you will find that you'll want to continue moving forward. The successful person you have created will just keep unrelentingly pulling you onward; it will not give up on you. The false ideas that had been holding you back will again and again be exposed as false; and when you quit believing them, they will just disappear. You will finally see more and more accurately the lovable, wonderful person you were when you were born, and you will move forward and demonstrate more of who you are.

> **Testimonial**
>
> "It's been more than two years since I first tried out Success by Emotions, and I highly recommend it.

"In 2022, I had been wanting to clean out a few closets in my home for several years but was making very little headway. I was working with Bob at the time, and he encouraged me to try out SBE. I agreed.

"It wasn't all smooth sailing for me, though it is for many people. When I tried to accumulate positive emotions to outweigh my inertia and feelings that I would never get the job done, it was difficult for me. I'm a well of feelings, but evoking specific ones on command felt phony to me, and I was resistant. I made an effort to reduce my resistance, and I chose a physical symbol of how I would be feeling upon achieving my goal to help me. But still, I couldn't get to the strong feelings that Bob had described.

"Over time, both Bob and I concluded that each person is different, and I'm wired in a way that accessing feelings on command is a harder ask. I lowered my expectations about the strength of my feelings, and I went for less intense emotions. Over time, I was able to summon enough to get me started. Once I started, the feelings of wanting to reach my goal grew. Over the next few months, I not only decluttered my closets to a large degree (not perfectly), but I also decluttered the rest of my home. Things tended to pile up again, and I continued to use SBE to get back on track as needed.

"I liked the cleaner, fresher feelings my decluttered home gave me, and I wanted more of them. About a year later, I replaced old carpet in a few places with hardwood, and I revamped my patio. I work from home, and my brain works better when my surroundings are aesthetically pleasing to me, and SBE helped me get closer to where I want to be. (I still have goals to accomplish for my home, but some of them cost money, so I do them as I'm able to afford them.)

"I think SBE is a remarkable tool that will help anyone who is willing to try it out, and I encourage you to do exactly that."

—Sue Bergin

An Added Benefit

By using SBE to become a better person, I felt more love for others and for myself, and this helped me achieve another goal I had been struggling with: losing weight.

I've included this topic toward the end of the book because it is something you should only attempt after you have successfully used SBE for a number of other goals; at that point, you will love yourself enough to make this change in a healthy and manageable way.

Remember, we are wired to act in the way we see ourselves. I had known for many years that I should lose some weight, but because I still saw myself at my current weight, the best I could do was maintain my weight. Then, after using SBE to make progress toward becoming a better person and loving myself more, I saw myself in a new light was able to use the tool to help me lose weight.

In the past, I had made no progress in this area of my life; I would lose some weight, but then I'd gain it all back. I had been using traditional growth, and my false ideas remained in place and in control. But now the approach would be very different.

Before, I had denied myself food to punish myself for overeating. There was not much joy in this. Now it was totally different. I set a goal and a completion date. I pictured myself sitting in a chair in my office, celebrating how I would be feeling for having maintained my weight loss for about six months. (Being in a different chair reminded me that this would be happening after I had succeeded at losing weight and after I had *maintained* that weight loss.) I then worked on accumulating enough emotions to believe I could succeed, convince myself I would succeed, and then come to know I would succeed. To get to this point took several hours of accumulating emotions spread over several days. I knew I had reached step four when I realized I was willing to do anything I needed to succeed.

I had some setbacks, but the successful version of myself that I had created kept pulling me forward. I was doing this from early November into mid-January, during the holiday season when I would have typically gained a few pounds. One day, I was feeling really frustrated, and this signaled to me that I had reached a major turning point. (See step three in chapter 4.) I suddenly realized that I was feeling frustrated because I had been keeping track of how much food I'd been eating. In other words, I was acting like a dieter. When we diet, we worry about how much we are eating, and we force ourselves to eat less. On the other hand, when we use SBE, we see

USING SBE TO BECOME A BETTER PERSON

ourselves as the person we will be after we have lost the weight, and we love that new version of ourselves more than we love food. In the past, I would shoot myself down by feeling that I deserved a treat. This time around, I instead spent more time accumulating emotions, and I eventually came to love myself enough that it became easy to eat like a person who weighed less. From there, I just kept seeing myself as the version of myself who had reached my goal weight. Eventually, I did reach my goal, and I've been able to maintain that weight while treating my body with love.

This was a process; it did not happen overnight. Loving myself enough to take better care of my body was a step in that process. But I also needed to take the time to use SBE. I needed to set a goal and a completion date. I then needed to accumulate enough emotions to change the way I saw myself. Eventually, my incredible mind adjusted my actions and my metabolism to help me weigh the weight I saw myself at, because my mind was working toward harmony with my new thoughts.

For your journey, I strongly advise against using SBE to lose weight until you have had five or ten successes in other areas. We all have so many emotions connected to our sizes, shapes, and weights, so this should be one of the last goals you work on. By then, you will know that SBE is working for you, and you will have the self-love you'll need to help you lose weight.

In the next chapter, I will outline some of the additional improvements I made by using SBE. The beauty of

SUCCESS BY EMOTIONS

this tool is that we can start with small goals. And, as we continue to accumulate emotions, we just keep moving forward.

SEVEN

Gaining More Peace

AS YOU'VE SEEN BY NOW, I have succeeded in using Success by Emotions to create significant results in many areas of my life. I have used it to strengthen my marriage and my relationship with my family, love myself and my body enough to easily and happily lose weight without hating and punishing myself, and increase my income to go from being bankrupt on paper at age thirty-three to being financially independent at age forty-four.

In the process of achieving these goals, SBE has allowed me to change the way I see myself. I have gone from seeing myself as someone who could not succeed to seeing myself as not only a winner but as someone who can hardly fail. In each of these moves forward, my results have far exceeded my expectations. And, by changing how I see myself, I have gained more peace than I ever imagined.

SUCCESS BY EMOTIONS

Gaining Peace

As you remove your false ideas, you will gain a better understanding of who you are. You will also gain the help of your incredible mind and assistance from the world around you. The combination of these three forces will enable you to do things that are far beyond anything you ever thought possible, and you will find more peace within yourself and in your life.

Using SBE enabled me to finally be at peace with who I am as a person. Previously, I had spent my life feeling discontent. I was competitive and was always working to be special. I did not enjoy what I was doing, because I always wanted to find a way to do it better. This drive to be special was rooted in my early days.

I have little recollection of the details of those years, but I do remember feeling a lot of confusion, fear, and insecurity. When I was born, my father was forty years old, and my mother was just a few months shy of turning forty. None of my four grandparents were living. On the day I was born, and for a time after my birth, my father was in a veteran's hospital in Wyoming undergoing electric shock treatments for post-traumatic stress disorder, which he experienced after serving in France during World War I. For a while after his return, he did quite well, but then his war experiences caught up with him again. The treatments ultimately did not work, and he spent the remainder of his eighty-nine-year life self-medicating with alcohol.

My mother had had a difficult childhood. Her mother had died when she was just eight years old. And, a few years later, she discovered her brother deceased in their basement. He had been electrocuted by a random power surge. She did not marry until she was twenty-eight years old, which was unusual for that time. Life with my father was difficult, and to protect herself from the pain of her earlier years and the pian of living with my father, she built an emotional wall around herself that kept her from experiencing or expressing feelings.

I was born in Salt Lake City, Utah, in 1936, during the low point of the Great Depression. I imagine that having a baby in the midst of all that financial turmoil was the last thing my mother wanted. She had to return to work immediately after my birth, and I was passed around to various babysitters.

These circumstances created a big problem for me. Having parents who were emotionally unavailable left me feeling neglected. I had caregivers, but they did not care for me like parents normally should have. All of this created feelings of abandonment that went deep into my soul. This pain became a part of my experience. Rather than just accept that my parents had done the best they could, I decided that I *was not worthy of love*, and that I had deserved to be abandoned. I also must have subconsciously followed my mother's example, and to protect myself from my pain, I built a wall that would keep me from feeling or communicating my emotions. And, if anyone tried to express love for me, my wall kept me from experiencing those feelings.

Then, as I grew older, I determined that, if I became special enough, I would never again be subject to abandonment; I would never feel that level of pain again. This caused me to become very competitive, to work very hard, be judgmental, create superior results, and never let anyone get close enough to me to hurt me. This damaged my relationships, especially those with my family.

Decades later, I have been able to use SBE to let go of the need to be special, and I've come to accept myself as a normal person with my own strengths and weaknesses. By doing this, I have finally gained a sense of peace within myself, just as I am.

The Spiral

While I was using SBE to let go of my need to be special, I discovered an important element to how our false ideas keep us stuck. Imagine your journey toward growth as a spiral, where your core false idea is at the center of the spiral, with many other supporting false ideas extending outward.

In using SBE, once you flip the scale toward truth, you are able to go directly to the center of the spiral and expose the core false idea that is holding you back. This causes your mind to eliminate that core idea. Once that core idea has been eliminated, all the supporting false ideas just fade away. This is a natural law, and it's what makes SBE so powerful. The hard work is having the

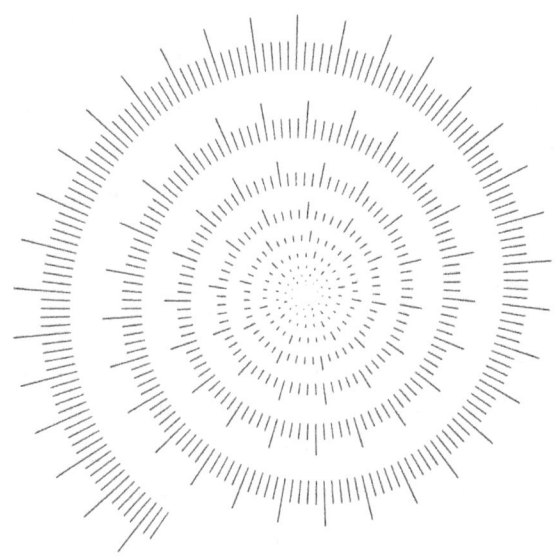

patience and determination to keep accumulating emotions until the core idea is eliminated.

By comparison, in most traditional approaches to personal growth, your supporting false ideas are eliminated after you have succeeded (and some are eliminated in the process of succeeding), but your core false idea remains. With that core idea still in place, you have to fight through the supporting ideas one at a time, from the outside of the spiral inward. This takes extra time and energy. If your spiral contains ten false ideas, then before you get to the core, your success is ten times harder.

In addition, in traditional growth, you sometimes go over and around your false ideas. They are not eliminated, and they come back repeatedly to slow you down. With

SBE, your lies and false ideas are permanently eliminated. This enables you to achieve your current goal and to also achieve all other future goals in that area of your life.

This is one big reason why I achieved success in business so rapidly when I used SBE, and it's why I had failed when I first tried to sell life insurance. Early on, I had so many false ideas to fight through that it wore me down, and I quit. The spiral was bigger than I could handle. But my second attempt—while using SBE—was entirely different. The truth of knowing that I would succeed eliminated my core false idea, and the remaining supporting false ideas just went away because the core was gone. It is impossible for a building to remain standing when the foundation is removed.

The same thing can happen for you. As you continue to use SBE and gain the additional truth you need to see yourself as more of the winner that you already are, you will use this additional truth to cut through the spiral and eliminate your core false idea, and the supporting false ideas will fall away as well. In this way, your path toward being at peace and content with who you are will become easier, faster, and more enjoyable.

Testimonial

"SBE is a very potent tool which taught me how to tap into the power of my emotions and harness them for self-improvement purposes. Before I heard about

SBE, I tended to think of emotions in relatively negative and shallow terms. I mistakenly assumed that problem-solving was primarily a function of harnessing my logical, rational brainpower. What I failed to recognize is that, many times, I don't know what I don't know. Therefore, attempting to solve a problem with a rational or logical solution is often wasteful, misguided, and frustrating. I also mistakenly assumed that many of my problems could be solved with sheer willpower.

"What SBE taught me is that there are incredible gains to be made by mentally leapfrogging the obstacle or dilemma that currently stands in my way, especially if the pathway to success is not obvious in the moment. It also taught me how to plant my feet on the other side of the obstacle, if only briefly at first, to establish some small measure of confidence that the reality of the other side does indeed exist and can be achieved. It's one thing to watch others succeed; it is altogether different to emotionally experience yourself succeeding, if only on a small scale. Personally, SBE revealed to me that my current perception of myself is not necessarily reality. I can recommend SBE for anyone who has come to the hard realization that willpower alone is not the answer to overcoming the self. There is a world of powerful emotion within us just waiting to be converted into an agent for change."

—Dave Ference

Uncovering Hidden False Ideas

Sometimes, our core false ideas are hidden, and we need outside help to see them before we can use SBE to eliminate them.

While I was working on letting go of my need to be special, my family was smart enough to suggest that I spend time seeing a therapist. I had been drafting this book for about three years, and my family could see that I was stuck. Luckily, I found an excellent therapist, and I spent about three hours a week with him.

During those six-plus months, he helped me see that I had a number of hidden false ideas, some of which had begun near the time of my birth. And my core false idea about needing to be special had become so strong that it had kept me from even seeing that I had these other false ideas. I had a problem, but I did not know I had a problem. I was not moving forward, and I did not know why, until I got outside help from my therapist.

Most of our false ideas are not known to us. And when we eliminate them through SBE, we do not even know when they are gone. We only know that our lives are working much better. That is our biggest evidence that there were hidden false ideas that have been eliminated.

This X-ray demonstrates a famous story that can help you understand the impact of our hidden false ideas.

In 1995, a British construction worker stepped on a six-inch nail which had been protruding upward out of a plank of wood. The nail pierced the bottom of his boot and continued, unabated, in its upward direction directly

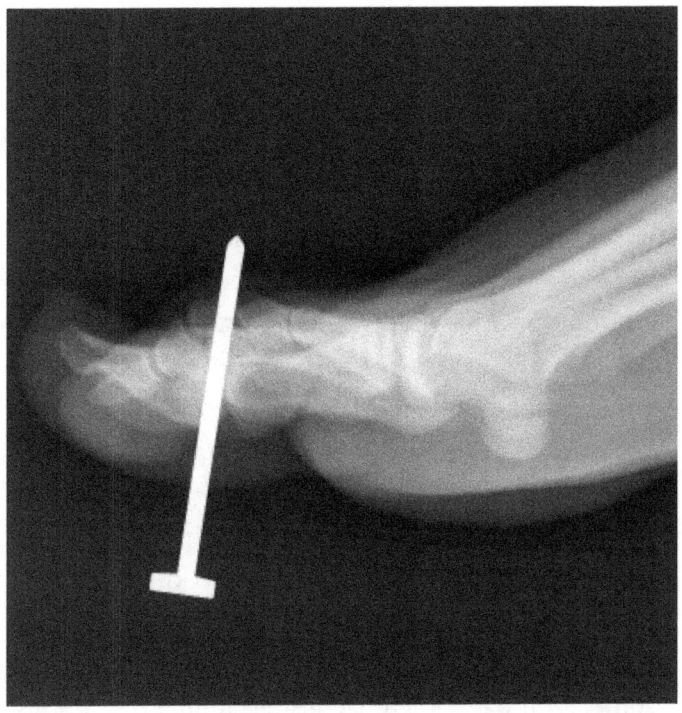

under the ball of his foot, slicing through the leather and exiting out of the top of his boot. The construction worker, writhing in intense pain, was rushed to a local hospital for immediate treatment. The pain was so intense that he was prescribed fentanyl, a very strong opioid painkiller, and midazolam, a sedative.

The medical team carefully removed his boot to treat the injury. To their surprise, they found that the nail had pierced his boot but had only lodged between his toes. It had not pierced his skin. The construction worker's boot had been damaged by the nail, but his foot was entirely unscathed.

This story illustrates a deep concept that applies to all of us: we may be living a lie, and we may be suffering the painful results of that lie.

Just like the construction worker who was in agony from an imagined injury, we have all, at some point in our lives, stepped on a metaphorical nail (our hidden false ideas) which has remained lodged in our boot. The pain from those false ideas takes control of our lives and holds us back. We do not remove the nail. Instead, we cut the plank of wood to match the size of our boot, and we relearn to walk with the boot permanently attached to the plank.

But it doesn't have to be this way. This is one of the great beauties of SBE. We do not need to know what our hidden false ideas are. But we do need to know where we could do better in our lives. With SBE, we set a goal and a completion date. Then, we just accumulate emotions. As we accumulate enough emotions, we will almost magically identify and expose the false ideas that had been holding us back—even the ones that we couldn't see. Once our false ideas are exposed, our minds let them go and they simply fade away. False ideas only exist for us as long as we believe in them.

Sometimes, the hidden lie is so big that we need to get outside help. That was my situation with the false ideas I had accumulated near the time of my birth. I needed a therapist to help me see that I had a nail in my boot. I was not even aware that it was there. I had cut the plank to be the size of my foot, and I had walked on it for over eighty years. I was so used to having this false idea with me that it had become part of who I was. I needed outside help to take off the boot and see that I was just fine, that I didn't need to be special to protect myself from abandonment. Once I could get the boot off and see the truth about my whole and complete self, I could go forward and find peace.

Being Human

As the therapist helped me identify my hidden false ideas, I was given the chance to use SBE to eliminate them. I set a goal to let go of needing to be special and move toward being human, with my own set of strengths and weaknesses.

First, my therapist would point out a hidden false idea. For example, I had believed that, if I ever stopped working at being special, the truth about me would be revealed. People would discover that I am not special, and I would again be abandoned. That was not true, but it was the fear that had been driving me. As long as that belief was in charge, I was forced to live in fear.

Then, together, we would uncover how I had protected myself from the pain of my early experiences. To get past the false ideas I had hidden, I had to be willing to first face the pain.

Prior to about age five, I had only one childhood memory. I can remember when we were on vacation in Oregon. I was cracking walnuts with a hammer when I hit my thumb with the hammer. I started to cry. My mother told me to think of a good thought and stop crying. My grandmother had been a Christian Science practitioner, and although my mother had not joined that faith, she used its principles to block out pain. As I grew older, I had built a similar wall to protect myself from pain.

Now, eighty years later, I was being told that I had to finish taking down that wall and reexperience all the pain of my past if I were to move forward. Before I could do this, I needed to move away from my need to be special and move toward being at peace with myself as a normal human being. I used SBE to do this, and I worked on accumulating the emotions I would feel in the weeks after I had made significant strides in this direction. In time, I had accumulated enough emotions to change the way I saw myself. Eventually, I gained more peace and freedom by seeing myself as someone who was just like everyone one else, someone with strengths and weaknesses. This gave me the courage to then take down some of my walls.

The spiral of false ideas I had created to support my need to be special was enormous. This ever-expanding spiral had kept me from seeing the other bigger lies that had been holding me back. If I had not had SBE (and outside help), I would have been overwhelmed. I could not have possibly lived long enough to take down those false ideas one at a time. Going step by step, from the outside of the spiral inward, would have seemed impossible. Even with the help of SBE and being able to attack the core false idea, the process still took time and effort.

Accomplishing this objective brought me so much peace. My need to be special had been so strong that it had controlled my life. Now I am moving closer to accepting myself for who I am, just like everyone I know. I have more strengths than weaknesses, and I am learning to embrace the fact that I have weaknesses ... because everyone has them.

In "The Strangest Secret," Earl Nightingale says, "Don't compete; create." For decades, my false belief that it was good to be special kept me from following the most important half of this statement. Back then, I was *creating* great ways to make money for my clients, and I was very creative in business. But I was *competing* all the time with everyone. I was always judging to see who was better or best. I always needed to do more and be more.

By using SBE to see myself as a normal person, with strengths and weaknesses, I was able to love others for their own unique sets of strengths and weaknesses. And this enabled me to follow the full meaning of Nightingale's statement. I began to better understand what he meant when he said, "Don't compete; create." The less we compete against others—and the more we focus instead on loving and serving others—the happier we are and the easier it is for us to love ourselves. And, in that love, we find peace.

When I was trying to compete with everyone else, I was stuck in the lie that I needed to be special. But when I accepted myself—with all of my flaws and strengths—I was able to turn my focus toward loving others and creating value for others. And, in turn, I found more peace within myself. This has taken time, and it is still something that I'm working on. I used SBE to set my goal and a completion date. I went through the four steps and made some progress. But again, the greatest growth came after my completion date as my love for myself and others has continued to grow. It has been a wonderful thing to experience.

I am now at peace with who I am and with my circumstances. At the same time, I know I still have many more false ideas to eliminate. But the process is now fun, and I am excited to keep doing it.

EIGHT

Sharing the Bounty

MY GOAL IS TO DISTRIBUTE this book to over one million individuals during the next two years. To accomplish this very aggressive objective, I will need your help. I need champions who will help me in helping others—especially young people—improve their lives and see better results.

Now that you've reached the final chapter of this book, I'm asking you to spend the five or six hours it will take to use the principles of Success by Emotions and create value in your own life so you can encourage others to use this tool.

I have spent more than four years creating this book so that it can benefit you and everyone else you will share it with. In that time, I have worked to understand SBE more fully so that it could help everyone, no matter what challenges they may be facing. And the rewards I have received in the process of doing this have been great.

Now I need readers—like you—to invest time in themselves so they can create results in their own lives and then help others create results in their lives. You will receive great rewards as you use SBE. But those rewards will pale in comparison with the joy you will receive as you enrich the lives of others by giving them the ability to accomplish their goals faster and easier than they ever thought possible. As it says on the book cover: *Achieve the impossible in half the time.*

If you have purchased this book, I hope you will purchase additional copies and give them to your friends. Or, you can invite them to receive the free e-book by entering their email address at https://www.successbyemotions.com/.

If you have received the e-book directly from me by email, please forward the email and the e-book to five or ten of your friends.

If someone has forwarded you the e-book, please pass it on to five or ten others.

Remember, when we were born, we each had a clear view of how wonderful and great we were (and still are). Then, as life happened, we accumulated false ideas that have kept us from seeing who we really are. These false ideas are hidden from our view, like the part of an iceberg that is underwater, lurking unseen. They are held in place by our emotions, and even though we cannot see them, they are holding us back. For the most part, we intellectually know what we need to do to achieve our goals. But the false ideas we have accumulated—and the emotions that hold them in place—hold their own power and keep us from doing many of the things we want to achieve.

Success by Emotions (SBE) is a tool that enables you to use your emotions to expose your false ideas. And, once they are exposed as false, your mind eliminates them.

The problem you may face right now is that your emotions may be telling you not to use this tool or share this book, as I have requested. In the past, you may have learned to make decisions based on logic, not emotions. Using emotions to solve a problem may still feel counterintuitive. Or, you may have some false ideas that are keeping you from using SBE because you fear failure. Perhaps you have failed in the past, and you're afraid you may fail again. Whatever may be holding you back, you can turn it around and use the power of your emotions to compel you toward more happiness and success rather than keeping you stuck.

As we've discussed, SBE is based on the natural laws that we each have our own unique set of false ideas, and that we can accumulate emotions to release those false ideas and improve our lives by knowing our true selves. It is like the law of gravity; it always works. But, to allow these laws to work for you, you need to keep accumulating emotions, even when you feel like giving up, until you expose and eliminate your false ideas.

For your first attempt at using SBE, please do not set a huge goal or objective. If you're feeling stuck and need a push to keep working at accumulating emotions, I suggest that you move to a goal that is easier to accomplish. Remember, our results are the hardest and take the longest to change. The next hardest to change are our actions. But changing our feelings and our ideas is much easier and faster. So pick one area of your life where you want to reconnect with the true potential you were born with. Once you see yourself as a success in that area of your life, it will build within you the desire to achieve other more difficult goals, and you will be starting with more faith in yourself and more faith in SBE.

"The Strangest Secret" is one of the best outlines for traditional growth that has ever been recorded. To my knowledge, since it was first released in 1953, it has sold more records than any other. Even though it was recorded in the middle of the last century, it still does a masterful job of helping us understand the incredible power of the human mind. But, for all of its timeless value, "The Strangest Secret" (like all methods of traditional growth) is very different from Success by Emotions.

With this book and the tool it introduces, we are making significant changes to traditional approaches to growth. In both traditional growth and SBE, we are asked to set a goal, establish a completion date, and select something that we will be doing after we have achieved our goal. And here is where SBE sets itself apart as a revolutionary new tool. In SBE, we are not working to become the person who can achieve our goal. We believe we are already that person, and we are using SBE to remove the false ideas that are keeping us from seeing the truth that we were born with all the talents and abilities we need to succeed.

To remove those false ideas, we use emotions combined with intellectual understanding to expose these false ideas. In both traditional growth and SBE, we intellectually believe we can achieve our goal; otherwise, we would not have chosen that goal. But, in using SBE, we recognize that the emotions that are holding our false ideas in place are telling us we cannot do it (or that doing it will be difficult to achieve). Those emotions are much too strong to be removed by intellectual arguments. We need to fight fire with fire. We need to use new, positive emotions to outweigh our existing negative emotions. We need SBE.

With SBE, we accumulate enough emotions to outweigh and expose the old emotions as false. Our emotions have more power over us than our intellectual reasoning. In SBE, we recognize this, and we accumulate emotions connected with how we will feel in the days, weeks, or months after we have achieved our goal. We then continue to accumulate these emotions until we can outweigh the emotions that are holding our false ideas in place. Once these false ideas are exposed as false, our minds have no further reason to hold on to them, and these false ideas are eliminated.

This is the hard part about using SBE. We need to keep accumulating emotions until we have gone through all four steps in the process. We need to accumulate enough emotions to believe we can succeed, then enough to convince ourselves that we can succeed, and then enough to know that we will succeed. When we know that we will succeed, we are willing to joyfully do whatever it takes to succeed.

Once this happens, our incredible minds and the world around us are free to help us succeed. At this point, it is only a matter of time until we will succeed. Whenever I reach this point in the process, I never worry about what might cause me to fail. If, by chance (and this has only rarely happened over the last fifty years), something happens to prevent me from succeeding, this is fine because the journey will have been a happy one, and I will have learned many things that will help me in the future.

There is another significant difference between traditional growth and SBE. With SBE, we do not need to do the thirty-day test presented in "The Strangest Secret." Instead, we utilize the habit of thinking and acting like successful people. When we face a setback, we do not try to use the thought of success to fight through the problem. We are already confident that we will succeed. A setback is not the end of the line; it is simply a learning experience. With this mindset, we pause to figure out what we can learn to be even more successful in the future, and we use SBE to feel how we will feel after we have learned this new way of being. In time, SBE becomes our knee-jerk reaction whenever we face a setback.

Another difference between SBE and traditional growth arises when we are fighting against the pull of our emotions, particularly when we are working to not do something that will harm us, or when we are working to avoid seeking something that is not in our best interest. We intellectually know it is not the best path to follow, but our emotions are drawing us down that path. If we continue to stuff our emotions, they can grow to the point that we end up acting on them. We cannot effectively use SBE to stop doing something; instead, we use it to help move us toward what we intellectually know is in our best interest.

If we use SBE and choose a goal that is better for us than the one our emotions are pulling us toward, we can then accumulate enough emotions to move through the four steps—and we accomplish two objectives. First, we gain more desire to achieve the objective that is better for us. Second, we gain enough truth to clearly understand why it is the better path to go down. This eliminates the power of our previously held false ideas and the emotions that were holding them in place.

This is why SBE has been so helpful to me in losing weight. I have gained so much love for myself and my body, and so much truth as to why being healthier will benefit my life, that I have learned to love my body more than I love food. This has made eating less and losing weight so much easier.

SUCCESS BY EMOTIONS

Even when we understand all of these reasons why SBE is so unique and so powerful, we can still sometimes find ourselves feeling discouraged throughout the process. This usually happens when we are not willing to keep trusting in SBE. If you ever find yourself getting impatient and you want things to go according to your timetable, remember that the most important benefits of using SBE are the happiness you gain and who you will become in the process; these are much more important than whatever you are able to accomplish or how quickly you can reach your goal. Rather than worrying about how long it's taking to achieve your goal, focus instead on eliminating your false ideas and moving yourself forward; let everything else unfold as it will. When you find you are not enjoying the journey, just pause and accumulate emotions. That will get you back on track. And, if that does not quickly help, then you can pause to learn what you need to learn to move forward.

Also remember that your successes will build upon each other over time, and the more you use SBE, the easier it will be to achieve bigger and bigger goals. With this tool in your hands, your potential truly is limitless.

It is my sincere wish that you will start using SBE and enjoying all of the many wonderful ways it will transform your life. I also hope you will soon be willing to forward this book to others, because I believe it will help them to find success and happiness in their journey forward. If anything is holding you back from doing either of these, you might consider using SBE to break through that resistance. You could set a goal to either use the tool or share the book, and then list the benefits that will come to you and the emotions you will feel by bringing yourself and others more happiness and a faster, easier path forward.

Final Comments

CONGRATULATIONS ON REACHING THE END of this book and beginning your incredible journey with Success by Emotions. I hope that this valuable tool will help you achieve your goals more quickly and easily—and, most importantly, that it will help you find more truth and peace in all areas of your life. To receive tips on how to get even more out of SBE, I encourage you to visit https://www.successbyemotions.com/ and enter your email address for regular updates.

In these early days, as you begin to use SBE, please remember that it is hard for us to do something new on our own. Finding encouragement from others can help keep you motivated to stick with the process. Tell someone what you are trying to do, so that they can give you support along the way. You can also report to them on your progress (or lack thereof). Being willing to connect and be vulnerable in this way will be freeing and very helpful.

As I mentioned earlier, in the beginning, it is better to stick with smaller, reasonable goals that intellectually make sense to you. Eventually, your successes will build your self-confidence. They will also build your trust and confidence in SBE. The improvements that you will make after achieving your first goal will far exceed your current expectations, and you will be able to achieve bigger and bigger goals each time you use SBE.

As you use SBE, you will likely discover things that I have not discussed in this book, things that will improve this book. I hope you will share them with me so that we can deepen our understanding of SBE together, and so that I can continue to revise the book for future editions. I would also like to hear your story of how you have improved your life using SBE. I will be sharing these testimonials online so that even more people can learn about the benefits of this incredible tool. To get in touch, email me at info@successbyemotions.com.

Sharing Success by Emotions

As I mentioned in the final chapter of this book, I would like to see over one million individuals benefit from SBE and enjoy its results. If you have found value in using SBE, I ask that you help me in distributing this book by sharing it with everyone you know. I want everyone to just keep forwarding it so it can reach as many

FINAL COMMENTS

people as possible. You can direct people to receive a free copy at https://www.successbyemotions.com/.

I want to help others use SBE to set goals, accumulate wonderful emotions, and expose and eliminate as many of their false ideas as possible and replace them with truth. I want to do the same for myself, too. As we do this together, we all move toward being more whole and complete, and our focus will be to love and be loved. When I watch my three-year-old great-grandchildren play together, I see that they are eager to help each other succeed and help each other find more happiness in their lives. That is what I hope this book will bring to the world.

We each will use SBE to accomplish different goals, and we each will remove many different false ideas. Our journeys will be different, but because we are using SBE, they will all be joyous. Knowing that this tool can help us be like little children full of love—willing to love others as they are now and willing to allow others to love as we are now—our shared objective will be to help each other move forward faster.

As I look back on everyone who has benefited from SBE over the past several decades, I feel a lot of love, appreciation, and support. I did not spend years doing research or studying to discover this tool. I simply listened to "The Strangest Secret" and then sat in a Porsche. The last four years I spent attempting to better understand SBE have improved my life in so many ways, and I am thankful for this experience. I am also very thankful for those who have opened their hearts and minds enough to try SBE. And I am thankful in advance for those who will use SBE in the future. Finally, I am thankful for you, for trusting in me and in the miraculous process of Success by Emotions.

I hope you are willing to let SBE improve your life. As I said in the beginning, it takes courage to try something new and different. But I know you have that courage within you, and the effort you put into using SBE will open up infinite potential for you. I wish you all the best for your ongoing success!

—Bob Raybould

About the Author

OVER THE COURSE OF FIVE decades as a successful salesman and businessman, Bob Raybould has utilized his self-improvement tool, Success by Emotions (SBE), to further his career and enrich his personal life.

In 1961, when the Berlin Wall went up, Bob served in Germany as the Report of Survey officer for the entire Seventh Army. In this role, he had unlimited power to either hold or relieve offenders accused of destroying or stealing government property. This meant that he was responsible for reviewing the work of colonels and lieutenant colonels who were four or five ranks higher than him. Asking these officers to modify their reports was (in a great understatement) challenging. After serving in that role for two years, he was awarded the Seventh Army Certificate of Achievement.

SUCCESS BY EMOTIONS

A few years later, while Bob was in the early stages of financial planning, he was given a great opportunity. In 1969, a change in the tax law enabled insurance companies to buy oil fields. In the past, these companies had lent money for the purchase of oil fields, and the new tax law eliminated such transactions. Bob's friend, Vince Allen, was one of the few people to recognize this opportunity, and he asked Bob to contact life insurance companies. Working with Vince and his company, Petro Search, Bob helped Aetna Life buy the first oil field ever purchased by an insurance company.

In the mid-1980s, Bob introduced the University of Utah football team to SBE and showed their players how to use the tool to improve their performance. Later, in 2004, the team's coach, Urban Meyer, asked Bob to work with six of his players during the offseason. Four of those players went on to play in the NFL. Bob also worked with about twenty-five players during Utah's undefeated season, which was a great experience for Bob, who is a sports junkie and an avid Utah fan.

Bob again brought the principles of SBE to the sports world when he helped a Utah basketball player named Johnnie Bryant (now the associate head coach for the Cleveland Cavaliers, and former associate head coach for the New York Knicks) increase his free-throw percentage. Bryant had made 80 percent during his junior year; during his senior year, after working with Bob in the offseason and using SBE, his percentage improved to 90 percent.

ABOUT THE AUTHOR

In 1987, Bob joined John T. Sweazey to form a mortgage banking firm, TRI Financial, which filled a great need when the financial crisis of the late 1980s put most savings and loan firms out of business. In 2003, TRI sold its almost $2 billion portfolio of loans to Pittsburgh National Bank, making great returns for their investors.

In the mid-1990s, Bob helped a group of former CIA employees create a data mining firm called DTM Research Inc., which provided services for several large corporations and was capable of mining data and producing results far above what was being done commercially at the time.

In 2000, Bob helped his son and his partner launch Arlington Value Management, a very successful investment firm that outperformed the market by over 8 percent for about twenty years.

Since 2010, Bob has invested in start-ups with great potential, particularly in the health-care innovation sector. He has invested in multiple companies focused on diagnostics and therapeutics, believing that their technologies can positively impact patients and global health for decades to come. One of these companies has developed a groundbreaking technology for the early detection of cancer, identifying the disease at the earliest possible stages. Another company has introduced several disruptive technologies, including one that stops invading pathogens from reproducing, and a point-of-care molecular diagnostics platform that detects and tracks the transmission of diseases globally. Bob's investments reflect his commitment to future generations, ensuring they will benefit from advanced medical technologies and improved health-care outcomes.

Over the last four years, Bob has been working to better understand SBE so that others can use it and double their speed in moving forward and achieving their goals. This book is a result of that work.

Blank SBE Sheets

ON THE FOLLOWING PAGES, YOU will find several blank SBE sheets. As you use SBE to accumulate emotions, you will likely be inspired to revise your goal, benefits, and/or emotions as they evolve throughout the process. For this reason, you may need to create several versions of your SBE sheet for each goal.

If you find yourself running low on SBE sheets, you can also photocopy the following pages and create additional copies so you can continue to explore new goals and tap into your unlimited potential!

• • • • • • • My SBE Sheet • • • • • • •

My Goal:

_____

_____

_____

Completion Date:

_____

Tactile Cue:

_____

> **REMEMBER ...**
> By continuing to accumulate more emotions, I am continuing to get a better view of my true self—and that person is gently pulling me forward.

BENEFITS:

    1.

    2.

    3.

EMOTIONS:

    1.

    2.

    3.

    4.

My SBE Sheet

My Goal:

_____

_____

_____

Completion Date:

_____

Tactile Cue:

_____

> **REMEMBER ...**
> By continuing to accumulate more emotions, I am continuing to get a better view of my true self—and that person is gently pulling me forward.

BENEFITS:

1.

2.

3.

EMOTIONS:

1.

2.

3.

4.

• • • • • • My SBE Sheet • • • • • •

My Goal:

_____

_____

_____

Completion Date:

_____

Tactile Cue:

_____

> **REMEMBER ...**
> By continuing to accumulate more emotions, I am continuing to get a better view of my true self—and that person is gently pulling me forward.

BENEFITS:

1.

2.

3.

EMOTIONS:

1.

2.

3.

4.

My SBE Sheet

My Goal:

_____

_____

_____

Completion Date:

_____

Tactile Cue:

_____

> **REMEMBER ...**
> By continuing to accumulate more emotions, I am continuing to get a better view of my true self—and that person is gently pulling me forward.

BENEFITS:

1.

2.

3.

EMOTIONS:

1.

2.

3.

4.

• • • • • • My SBE Sheet • • • • • •

My Goal:

_____

_____

_____

Completion Date:

_____

Tactile Cue:

_____

> **REMEMBER ...**
> By continuing to accumulate more emotions, I am continuing to get a better view of my true self—and that person is gently pulling me forward.

BENEFITS:

    1.

    2.

    3.

EMOTIONS:

    1.

    2.

    3.

    4.

• • • • • • My SBE Sheet • • • • • •

My Goal:

_____

_____

_____

Completion Date:

_____

Tactile Cue:

_____

> **REMEMBER ...**
> By continuing to accumulate more emotions, I am continuing to get a better view of my true self—and that person is gently pulling me forward.

BENEFITS:

   1.

   2.

   3.

EMOTIONS:

   1.

   2.

   3.

   4.

My SBE Sheet

My Goal:

_____

_____

_____

Completion Date:

_____

Tactile Cue:

_____

> **REMEMBER ...**
> By continuing to accumulate more emotions, I am continuing to get a better view of my true self—and that person is gently pulling me forward.

BENEFITS:

1.

2.

3.

EMOTIONS:

1.

2.

3.

4.

My SBE Sheet

My Goal:

_____

_____

_____

Completion Date:

_____

Tactile Cue:

_____

> **REMEMBER ...**
> By continuing to accumulate more emotions, I am continuing to get a better view of my true self—and that person is gently pulling me forward.

BENEFITS:

1.

2.

3.

EMOTIONS:

1.

2.

3.

4.

My SBE Sheet

My Goal:

_____

_____

_____

Completion Date:

_____

Tactile Cue:

_____

> **REMEMBER ...**
> By continuing to accumulate more emotions, I am continuing to get a better view of my true self—and that person is gently pulling me forward.

BENEFITS:

    1.

    2.

    3.

EMOTIONS:

    1.

    2.

    3.

    4.

My SBE Sheet

My Goal:

_____

_____

_____

Completion Date:

_____

Tactile Cue:

_____

> **REMEMBER ...**
> By continuing to accumulate more emotions, I am continuing to get a better view of my true self—and that person is gently pulling me forward.

BENEFITS:

1.

2.

3.

EMOTIONS:

1.

2.

3.

4.

My SBE Sheet

My Goal:

_____

_____

_____

Completion Date:

_____

Tactile Cue:

_____

> **REMEMBER ...**
> By continuing to accumulate more emotions, I am continuing to get a better view of my true self—and that person is gently pulling me forward.

BENEFITS:

1.

2.

3.

EMOTIONS:

1.

2.

3.

4.

My SBE Sheet

My Goal:

_____
_____
_____

Completion Date:

_____

Tactile Cue:

_____

> **REMEMBER ...**
> By continuing to accumulate more emotions, I am continuing to get a better view of my true self—and that person is gently pulling me forward.

BENEFITS:

1.

2.

3.

EMOTIONS:

1.

2.

3.

4.

• • • • • • • My SBE Sheet • • • • • • •

My Goal:

_____

_____

_____

Completion Date:

_____

Tactile Cue:

_____

> **REMEMBER ...**
> By continuing to accumulate more emotions, I am continuing to get a better view of my true self—and that person is gently pulling me forward.

BENEFITS:

    1.

    2.

    3.

EMOTIONS:

    1.

    2.

    3.

    4.

My SBE Sheet

My Goal:

_____

_____

_____

Completion Date:

_____

Tactile Cue:

_____

> **REMEMBER ...**
> By continuing to accumulate more emotions, I am continuing to get a better view of my true self—and that person is gently pulling me forward.

BENEFITS:

1.

2.

3.

EMOTIONS:

1.

2.

3.

4.

My SBE Sheet

My Goal:

_____

_____

Completion Date:

_____

Tactile Cue:

_____

> **REMEMBER ...**
> By continuing to accumulate more emotions, I am continuing to get a better view of my true self—and that person is gently pulling me forward.

BENEFITS:

    1.

    2.

    3.

EMOTIONS:

    1.

    2.

    3.

    4.

My SBE Sheet

My Goal:

_____

_____

_____

Completion Date:

_____

Tactile Cue:

_____

> **REMEMBER ...**
> By continuing to accumulate more emotions, I am continuing to get a better view of my true self—and that person is gently pulling me forward.

BENEFITS:

1.

2.

3.

EMOTIONS:

1.

2.

3.

4.

My SBE Sheet

My Goal:

_____

_____

_____

Completion Date:

_____

Tactile Cue:

_____

> **REMEMBER ...**
> By continuing to accumulate more emotions, I am continuing to get a better view of my true self—and that person is gently pulling me forward.

BENEFITS:

1.

2.

3.

EMOTIONS:

1.

2.

3.

4.

www.ingramcontent.com/pod-product-compliance
Lightning Source LLC
Chambersburg PA
CBHW070318010526
44107CB00004B/349